SpringerBriefs in Business Process Management

Series editor

Jan vom Brocke, Vaduz, Liechtenstein

More information about this series at http://www.springer.com/series/13170

Ronny S. Mans · Wil M.P. van der Aalst
Rob J.B. Vanwersch

Process Mining in Healthcare

Evaluating and Exploiting Operational
Healthcare Processes

 Springer

Ronny S. Mans
Eindhoven University of Technology
Eindhoven
The Netherlands

Rob J.B. Vanwersch
Maastricht University Medical Center
Maastricht
The Netherlands

Wil M.P. van der Aalst
Eindhoven University of Technology
Eindhoven
The Netherlands

ISSN 2197-9618   ISSN 2197-9626   (electronic)
SpringerBriefs in Business Process Management
ISBN 978-3-319-16070-2   ISBN 978-3-319-16071-9   (eBook)
DOI 10.1007/978-3-319-16071-9

Library of Congress Control Number: 2015932849

Springer Cham Heidelberg New York Dordrecht London

Printed on acid-free paper

Springer International Publishing AG Switzerland is part of Springer Science+Business Media
(www.springer.com)

Acknowledgments

This research is supported by the Dutch Technology Foundation STW, Applied Science Division of NWO, and the Technology Program of the Ministry of Economic Affairs. The results were only possible due to the spectacular innovations in process mining over the last decade. Moreover, we heavily rely on powerful processes mining software (in particular ProM) that require major development efforts. We thank all "process mining enthusiasts" who contributed to the above.

Contents

About the Authors

Ronny S. Mans is a postdoctoral researcher at the Eindhoven University of Technology (TU/e). He is working in the Technology Foundation STW project "Developing Tools for Understanding Healthcare Processes" in which he focuses on the development of process mining techniques. He has published 10 journal papers, 30 refereed conference/workshop publications, and 8 book chapters. Ronny is a member of the editorial board of the KR4HC/ProHealth workshop and of the editorial board of the International Journal of Privacy and Health Information Management.

Wil M.P. van der Aalst is a full professor of Information Systems at TU/e. He is also the Academic Supervisor of the International Laboratory of Process-Aware Information Systems of the National Research University, Higher School of Economics in Moscow. Moreover, since 2003 he has a part-time appointment at Queensland University of Technology (QUT). His research interests include workflow management, process mining, Petri nets, business process management, process modeling, and process analysis. Wil has published more than 160 journal papers, 17 books (as author or editor), 300 refereed conference/workshop publications, and 50 book chapters. Many of his papers are highly cited (he has an H-index of 113 according to Google Scholar) and his ideas have influenced researchers, software developers, and standardization committees working on process support. He is also a member of the Royal Netherlands Academy of Arts and Sciences (KNAW), the Royal Holland Society of Sciences and Humanities (Koninklijke Hollandsche Maatschappij der Wetenschappen), and the Academy of Europe (Academia Europaea).

Rob J.B. Vanwersch is a program manager at Maastricht University Medical Center. In addition, he is a doctoral candidate and guest-lecturer within the Information Systems Group of the Department of Industrial Engineering and Innovation Sciences at TU/e. His research focuses on developing methodological support for redesigning business processes in health care. Rob Vanwersch has published several peer-reviewed journal and conference papers, and he is also a member of the user committee of the Technology Foundation STW project "Developing tools for understanding healthcare processes."

Chapter 1
Introduction

Abstract Healthcare costs have increased dramatically and the demand for high-quality care will only grow in our aging society. At the same time, more event data are being collected about care processes. Healthcare Information Systems (HIS) have hundreds of tables with patient-related event data. Therefore, it is quite natural to exploit these data to improve care processes while reducing costs. Data science techniques will play a crucial role in this endeavor. Process mining can be used to improve compliance and performance while reducing costs. The chapter sets the scene for process mining in healthcare, thus serving as an introduction to this *SpringerBrief*.

Keywords Healthcare information systems · Process mining · Healthcare · Business process management

Process mining has been applied successfully in a variety of domains, e.g., banking, insurance, logistics, production, e-government, customer relationship management, remote monitoring, and smart diagnostics. Through process mining one can relate the actual behavior of people, machines, and organizations with modeled behavior. This often leads to surprising insights showing that reality is very different from perceptions, opinions, and beliefs stakeholders have. This is particularly relevant for healthcare processes. These processes are often only partly structured with many exceptional behaviors and different stakeholders. Healthcare requires flexibility and ad-hoc decision making. These characteristics make it impossible to apply rigorous Business Process Management (BPM), Workflow Management (WFM), and Business Process Reengineering (BPR) techniques. Clearly, a hospital is not a factory and patients cannot be cured using a conveyor belt system. However, the abundance of data collected in today's hospitals can be used to improve care processes dramatically. Unlike many other domains, there is still room for dramatic improvements in healthcare processes. Process mining can be used to improve compliance and performance while reducing costs. To set the scene, this chapter introduces the application of process mining in healthcare. Section 1.1 discusses the main challenges in healthcare. In Sect. 1.2, process mining is positioned in the broader *data science* context. Subsequently, Sect. 1.3 discusses the application of process mining in healthcare. Section 1.4 concludes the chapter with an outlook on the remainder of this *SpringerBrief*.

R.S. Mans et al., *Process Mining in Healthcare*,
SpringerBriefs in Business Process Management, DOI 10.1007/978-3-319-16071-9_1

1.1 Challenges in Healthcare

Healthcare is facing several challenges. Some of the most urgent challenges become evident when looking at Fig. 1.1. First, at the top of the figure, it is shown that healthcare costs continue to rise. So, there is a need to reduce these costs. Second, the people receiving care are becoming older. This is likely to lead to greater demand for elderly care [1]. Finally, the bottom of the figure shows that the volume of long-term

Fig. 1.1 Within healthcare, costs are rising, people are aging, and the demand for care is increasing. **a** Total health expenditure as a share of GDP, 2000–2011. *Source* OECD Health Statistics 2013, http://dx.doi.org/10.1787/health-data-en. **b** Trends in the share of the population aged over 80 years, 1960–2050. *Source* OECD Historical Population Data and Projections Database, 2013. **c** Share of long-term care recipients aged 65 years and over receiving care at home, 2000 and 2011 (or nearest year). *Source* OECD Health Statistics 2013, http://dx.doi.org/10.1787/health-data-en

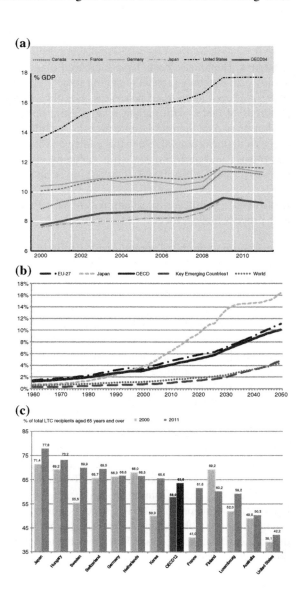

care increased in the period of 2000 till 2011. For these and the other types of care, further increases are expected. Regarding the care provided, an important health policy issue in many OECD countries relates to long waiting times [2]. These long waiting times cause dissatisfaction as the benefits of treatment are postponed.

The developments shown in Fig. 1.1 illustrate the pressure on today's healthcare organizations. They need to improve productivity and reduce access and waiting times while at the same time reducing costs. One approach to this is to focus on the many complex time-consuming and non-trivial processes that are undertaken within these organizations. Examples of such processes are the preparation and execution of a surgery and the treatment of patients suffering from cancer. In order to give suggestions for improving and redesigning these processes they need to be analyzed. Such an analysis is typically done by conducting interviews. Unfortunately, this is time consuming and costly. Furthermore, typically a *subjective* view is provided on how a process is executed. That is, people involved in the performance of these healthcare processes (e.g., physicians, managers) tend to have an ideal scenario in mind, which in reality is only one of the many scenarios possible. Moreover, in many hospitals "political battles" take place due to organizational issues. Different stakeholders may have different views, e.g., some parties may not be interested in reducing the overall costs and improving transparency. Therefore, in order to give objective suggestions for improving and redesigning processes one needs to exploit the event data readily available. Such an analysis is possible using process mining.

1.2 Process Mining: Data Science in Action

Although our capabilities to store and process data have been increasing exponentially since the 1960-ties, suddenly many organizations realize that survival is not possible without exploiting available data intelligently. This of course also holds for healthcare organizations. Society, organizations, and people are "Always On". Data are collected *about anything, at any time*, and *at any place* [3]. Gartner uses the phrase "The Nexus of Forces" to refer to the convergence and mutual reinforcement of four interdependent trends: social, mobile, cloud, and information [4]. The term "Big Data" is often used to refer to the incredible growth of data in recent years. For hospitals of course the goal is *not* to collect more data, but to exploit data *to realize more efficient and effective care processes*.

Obviously, the term "Big Data" has been hyped in recent years. However, there is rapidly growing demand for *data scientists* that can turn data into value. Just like computer science emerged as a new discipline from mathematics when computers became abundantly available, we now see the birth of data science as a new discipline driven by the huge amounts of data available today. Data science aims to use the different data sources to answer questions that can be grouped into the following four categories:

- Reporting: *What happened?*
- Diagnosis: *Why did it happen?*
- Prediction: *What will happen?*
- Recommendation: *What is the best that can happen?*

So, what is a data scientist? Many definitions have been suggested. For example, [5] states "Data scientists are the people who understand how to fish out answers to important business questions from today's tsunami of unstructured information". It is not easy to define the ideal profile of a data scientist. Clearly, data science is multidisciplinary. As Fig. 1.2 shows, data science is more than analytics/statistics. It also involves behavioral/social sciences (e.g., for ethics and understanding human behavior), industrial engineering (e.g., to value data and know about new business models), and visualization. Just like Big Data is more than MapReduce, data science is more than mining. Besides having theoretical knowledge of analysis methods, the data scientist should be creative and able to realize solutions using IT. Moreover, the data scientist should have domain knowledge and able to convey the message well. Figure 1.2 shows a possible profile of the data scientist: different subdisciplines are combined to render an engineer that has quantitative and technical skills, is creative and communicative, and is able to realize end-to-end solutions.

Figure 1.2 deliberately emphasizes the *process* aspect. The goal is not to analyze data, but to improve care processes. *Process mining* aims to *discover, monitor and improve real processes by extracting knowledge from event logs* readily available in today's information systems [6]. Starting point for process mining is an *event log*. Each event in such a log refers to an *activity* (i.e., a well-defined step in some process) and is related to a particular *case* (i.e., a *process instance*). The events

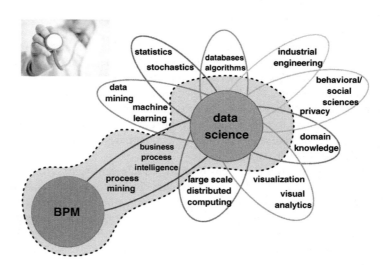

Fig. 1.2 Data science skills that should be combined to realize more efficient and effective care processes

belonging to a case are *ordered* and can be seen as one "run" of the process. Event logs may store additional information about events. In fact, whenever possible, process mining techniques use extra information such as the *resource* (i.e., person or device) executing or initiating the activity, the *timestamp* of the event, or *data elements* recorded with the event (e.g., the age of a patient).

Process mining bridges the gap between traditional model-based process analysis (e.g., simulation and other business process management techniques) and data-centric analysis techniques such as machine learning and data mining [6]. Process mining seeks the confrontation between event data (i.e., observed behavior) and process models (hand-made or discovered automatically). This technology has become available only recently, but it can be applied to any type of operational processes (organizations and systems).

There are three main types of process mining:

- The first type of process mining is *discovery*. A discovery technique takes an event log and produces a process model without using any a-priori information. An example is the Alpha-algorithm [7] that takes an event log and produces a process model (a Petri net) explaining the behavior recorded in the log.
- The second type of process mining is *conformance*. Here, an existing process model is compared with an event log of the same process. Conformance checking can be used to check if reality, as recorded in the log, conforms to the model and vice versa [8].
- The third type of process mining is *enhancement*. Here, the idea is to extend or improve an existing process model using information about the actual process recorded in some event log [6]. Whereas conformance checking measures the alignment between model and reality, this third type of process mining aims at changing or extending the a-priori model. An example is the extension of a process model with performance information, e.g., showing bottlenecks.

Process mining techniques can be used in an offline, but also online, setting. The latter is known as *operational support*. An example is the detection of non-conformance at the moment the deviation actually takes place. Another example is time prediction for running cases, i.e., given a partially executed case the remaining processing time is estimated based on historic information of similar cases.

1.3 Applying Process Mining to Healthcare Processes

As mentioned in Sect. 1.1 care organizations are under incredible pressure "to do more for less". To be able to improve processes it is important to understand what is really happening (process discovery) and analyze deviations from the expected or normative process model (conformance checking). Moreover, using the timestamps of events one can identify and diagnose bottlenecks and other inefficiencies (enhancement). Chapter 3 introduces process mining in detail. At this stage it is sufficient to have a rough idea of the results and insights provided by process mining.

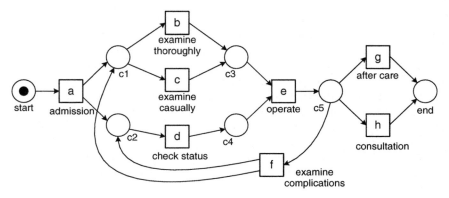

Fig. 1.3 Process model only showing the control-flow. The model is not intended to be realistic and only aims to show the different control-flow constructs in a healthcare setting

Figure 1.3 shows a simplified process model learned from event data. The backbone of the process model is formed by the control-flow, i.e., the ordering of activities. The control-flow is represented in terms of a Petri net, i.e., a bipartite graph of transitions representing activities and places representing states. The process starts by admitting a patient. This activity is modeled by transition *admission*. Each transition is represented by a square. Transitions are connected through places that model possible states of the process. Each place is represented by a circle. In a Petri net a transition is *enabled*, i.e., the corresponding activity can occur, if all input places hold a token. Transition *admission* has only one input place (start) and this place initially contains a token representing a patient that needs treatment. Hence, the corresponding activity is enabled and can occur. This is also referred to as *firing*. When firing, the transition consumes one token from each of its input places and produces one token for each of its output places. Hence, the firing of transition *admission* results in the removal of the token from input place *start* and the production of two tokens: one for output place *c1* and one for output place *c2*. Tokens are shown as black dots. The configuration of tokens over places—in this case the state of the patient's treatment—is referred to as *marking*. Figure 1.3 shows the initial marking consisting of one token in place *start*. The marking after firing transition *admission* has two tokens: one in place *c1* and one in place *c2*. After firing transition *admission*, three transitions are enabled. The token in place *c2* enables transition *check status*. This transition models a review of the medical history of the patient. In parallel, the token in *c1* enables both *examine thoroughly* and *examine casually*. Firing *examine thoroughly* will remove the token from *c1*, thus disabling *examine casually*. Similarly, the concurrence of *examine casually* will disable *examine thoroughly*. In other words, there is an exclusive choice between these two activities. Transition *examine thoroughly* is executed for patients where complications are expected. Less problematic cases only need a casual examination. Firing *check status* does not disable any other transition, i.e., it can occur concurrently with examine thoroughly or examine casually. Transition *operate* is only enabled if both input places contain a token. The medical history of patient needs to be checked beforehand (token in place *c4*) and the casual or thorough examination should have been completed (token in place *c3*). Hence, the process synchronizes before operating. Transition *operate* consumes two tokens and produces one token for *c5*. Three transitions share *c5* as an input place. This shows that there are three possible scenarios. Etc. The process ends with a token in place *end*.

A process model such as the one shown in Fig. 1.3 can be learned by analyzing events logs describing the activities executed for patients [6]. A possible *trace* for a particular patient is $\langle a, b, d, e, h \rangle$. Note that here we are using short names (e.g., $a = admission$) and do not show the attributes of the various events, e.g., timestamp, resource, and data. Another possible trace is $\langle a, c, d, e, f, d, c, e, f, c, d, e, h \rangle$. An event log can be viewed as a multiset of traces (if we ignored timestamps, etc.). $L = [\langle a, b, d, e, h \rangle^5, \langle a, d, c, e, g \rangle^4, \langle a, c, d, e, f, b, d, e, g \rangle^4, \langle a, d, b, e, h \rangle^3, \langle a, c, d, e, f, d, c, e, f, c, d, e, h \rangle^2, \langle a, c, d, e, g \rangle^2]$ is an event log with 20 cases. Based on this event log most process discovery techniques construct a control-flow model as is shown in Fig. 1.3. This model is indeed able to reproduce the traces observed.

The events belonging to a case are not just ordered. There may be extra information such as the resource (i.e., physician or nurse) executing or initiating the activity, the timestamp of the event, or data elements characterizing the patient. By replaying the event log on the model shown in Fig. 1.3 we can learn additional perspectives and enrich the model as is shown in Fig. 1.4.

As Fig. 1.4 shows, the process model can be extended with additional perspectives: the organizational perspective ("What are the organizational roles and which resources are performing particular activities?"), the case perspective ("Which characteristics of a case influence a particular decision?"), and the time perspective ("Where are the bottlenecks in my process?") [6]. Analysis of the event log shown may reveal that Sara is the only one performing the activities *operate* and *examine complications*. This suggests that there is a "surgeon role" and that Sara is the only one having this role. Activity *examine thoroughly* is performed only by Sue and Sean. This suggests some "physician role" associated to this activity, etc. Techniques for organizational process mining [6, 9] will discover such organizational structures and relate activities to resources through roles. By exploiting resource information in the log, the organizational perspective can be added to the process model. Similarly, information on timestamps and frequencies can be used to add performance related information to the model. Figure 1.4 sketches that it is possible to measure the time that passes between an examination (activities *b* or *c*) and the actual operation (activity *e*). If this time is remarkably long, process mining can be used to identify the problem and discover possible root causes. If the event log contains case-related information, this can be used to further analyze the decision points in the process. For instance, through decision point analysis it may be learned that older patients require multiple operations.

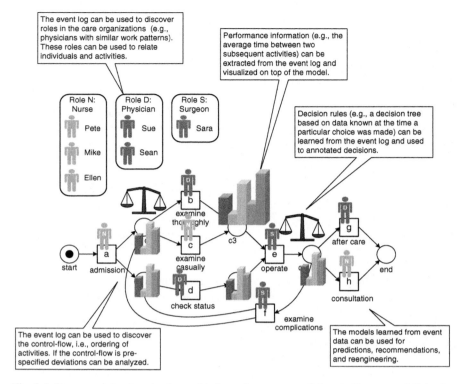

The event log can be used to discover roles in the care organizations (e.g., physicians with similar work patterns). These roles can be used to relate individuals and activities.

Performance information (e.g., the average time between two subsequent activities) can be extracted from the event log and visualized on top of the model.

Decision rules (e.g., a decision tree based on data known at the time a particular choice was made) can be learned from the event log and used to annotated decisions.

The event log can be used to discover the control-flow, i.e., ordering of activities. If the control-flow is pre-specified deviations can be analyzed.

The models learned from event data can be used for predictions, recommendations, and reengineering.

Fig. 1.4 Process mining is not only used to learn the process as it is actually executed: It is also used to understand deviations, to analyze bottlenecks, and to monitor organizational behavior

1.4 Outlook

Process mining [6] aims at extracting process knowledge from so-called *event logs* which may originate from all kinds of systems. Examples of such systems are Hospital Information Systems (HIS) but may also be systems in use at an intensive care storing all diagnostic tests and treatments that have been performed or a laboratory system storing all tests that have been performed on a blood sample. Typically, these event logs contain information about the start/completion of process steps together with related context data (e.g., actors and costs involved). Since process mining uses factual execution data, it allows for obtaining an objective view on how processes are really executed. In this way, there is a clear difference between process mining and more traditional ways of investigating business processes. For example, by conducting interviews there is always the risk that highly subjective information is gathered.

As process mining allows for easily getting insights into the real execution of organizational healthcare processes, not surprisingly, there is a growing uptake of the technique in the healthcare domain. That is, the obtained insights can be used for example to reduce costs and to improve the efficiency of the care processes. As part of this, the patient satisfaction is expected to grow. Also, in literature, up to now, we have discovered 59 publications in which a real-life application of process mining in healthcare is described (see http://www.healthcare-analytics-process-mining.org/ for an overview). For these applications often only data are taken from one or two systems in order to solve a particular problem. Despite this popularity, *an overview is missing of all the process related data that exists within a HIS*. As a result, it is difficult to *reason about potential applications of process mining within hospitals*.

The aforementioned two limitations and the uptake of process mining in the healthcare domain have been the reason for writing this *SpringerBrief* about process mining in healthcare. To this end, we present a *healthcare reference model* which outlines all the different classes of data that are potentially available for process mining and the relationships between these classes. Given this reference model, it is possible to reason about application opportunities for process mining, e.g., we will discuss several kinds of analyses that can be performed. This enables us to answer the following question: *What are the potential applications of process mining within hospitals?*

When applying process mining in hospitals, typically several data quality issues need to be tackled. For example, problems may exist related to timestamps in event logs, imprecise activity names, and missing events. Therefore, we also elaborate on *data quality issues*. In total 27 quality issues that may hamper the analysis of care processes based on event data were identified. We also provide *guidelines* to overcome these problems.

In the remainder, we provide an extensive overview of the issues and opportunities related to applying process mining in the healthcare domain. As such, a basis is provided for governing and improving the processes within a hospital.

Figure 1.5 shows an overview of this *SpringerBrief*. Starting point is a HIS (or similar system) that is supporting healthcare professionals. The healthcare reference model describes over 120 classes of information stored in a typical HIS. The reference model facilitates the search for relevant data and the ETL (Extract, Transform and Load) process. The resulting event logs can be used by a wide range of process discovery algorithms. For example, process models may be discovered that show what actually happens thus providing valuable insights. Existing artifacts like guidelines can be combined with event data to diagnose deviations. Opportunities to further exploit event data are endless, e.g., detecting bottlenecks or predicting capacity problems.

The remainder of this *SpringerBrief* is organized as follows. Chapter 2 discusses what kinds of healthcare processes can be analyzed using process mining. Therefore, a classification of healthcare processes is presented which gives an overview of the kinds of processes that can be found within the healthcare domain. Next, in Chap. 3 an introduction to process mining is given. In Chap. 4, the *healthcare reference model* is introduced. In Chap. 5, based on the reference model, the possibilities of process mining within a typical hospital will be illustrated. Chapter 6 lists common data quality issues and provides guidelines for logging. Finally, in Chap. 7 a short

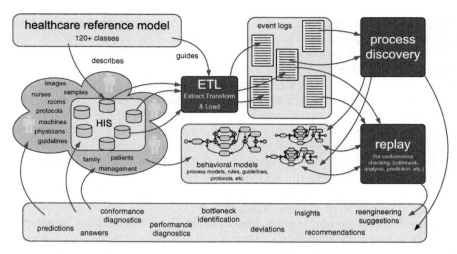

Fig. 1.5 Process mining in healthcare. Note that the healthcare reference model is used as a starting point for locating the data and extracting event logs

summary is given. Also, a vision for the application of process mining in healthcare based on the findings in this *SpringerBrief* is provided.

References

1. OECD. *Health at a Glance 2013: OECD Indicators*. OECD Publishing, 2013
2. L. Siciliani, M. Borowitz, and V. Moran. Waiting Time Policies in the Health Sector: What Works? Technical report, OECD Health Policy Studies, OECD Publishing, 2013
3. W.M.P. van der Aalst. Data Scientist: The Engineer of the Future. In K. Mertins, F. Benaben, R. Poler, and J. Bourrieres, editors, *Proceedings of the I-ESA Conference*, volume 7 of *Enterprise Interoperability*, pages 13–28. Springer, 2014
4. C. Howard, D.C. Plummer, Y. Genovese, J. Mann, D.A. Willis, and D.M. Smith. The Nexus of Forces: Social, Mobile, Cloud and Information. http://www.gartner.com, 2012
5. T.H. Davenport and D.J. Patil. Data Scientist: The Sexiest Job of the 21st Century. *Harvard Business Review*, pages 70–76, October 2012
6. W.M.P. van der Aalst. *Process Mining: Discovery, Conformance and Enhancement of Business Processes*. Springer-Verlag, Berlin, 2011
7. W.M.P. van der Aalst, A.J.M.M. Weijters, and L Maruster. Workflow Mining: Discovering Process Models from Event Logs. *IEEE Transactions on Knowledge and Data Engineering*, 16(9):1128–1142, 2004
8. W.M.P. van der Aalst, A. Adriansyah, and B.F. van Dongen. Replaying History on Process Models for Conformance Checking and Performance Analysis. *WIREs Data Mining and Knowledge Discovery*, 2(2):182–192, 2012
9. M. Song and W.M.P. van der Aalst. Towards Comprehensive Support for Organizational Mining. *Decision Support Systems*, 46(1):300–317, 2008

Chapter 2
Healthcare Processes

Abstract Process mining can be used to improve compliance and performance in hospitals and other care organizations. Before analyzing event data, we first provide an overview of the different types of care processes. We distinguish three levels of care: primary, secondary, and tertiary. We characterize five types of healthcare processes and link these to four basic types of data science questions: (a) What happened?, (b) Why did it happen?, (c) What will happen?, and (d) What is the best that can happen? Such questions can be answered using process mining. Using the characteristics of care processes, different questions may be posed. For example, the level of variability may influence the selection of the most suitable process mining technique.

Keywords Taxonomy of healthcare processes · Process mining · Healthcare · Data science · Characterizing healthcare processes

Healthcare can be seen as the diagnosis, treatment, and prevention of diseases in order to improve a person's wellbeing. Although healthcare is typically associated to hospitals, there are many care processes in other types of organizations. Various professionals may be involved in these processes. Examples of such professionals are general practitioners, dentists, midwives, and physiotherapists. Also, care is provided at home, rehabilitation centers, and nursing homes. Next to that, when looking at literature, typically it is indicated that healthcare processes are highly dynamic, complex, ad-hoc, and are increasingly multi-disciplinary [1]. Nevertheless, processes of different complexity and duration (up to several months) can be identified. This chapter provides a brief characterization of the spectrum of care processes encountered.

2.1 Different Levels of Care

Obviously, many different kinds of healthcare processes exist having different execution characteristics. Therefore, in this chapter, we focus on indicating which kinds of healthcare processes exist and the typical process characteristics that distinguish these processes. In the end, a classification is provided outlining the main kinds of healthcare processes.

© The Author(s) 2015
R.S. Mans et al., *Process Mining in Healthcare*,
SpringerBriefs in Business Process Management, DOI 10.1007/978-3-319-16071-9_2

Regarding the organization of care, there is a distinction into three levels of care. Each level corresponds to particular patient needs [2]. First, *primary care* involves common health problems (e.g. sore throats and hypertension) and preventive measures (e.g. vaccinations or electrocardiography) that account for 80–90 % of visits to a physician or other caregiver. So, primary care refers to the work of healthcare professionals who act as a first point of consultation for all patients within the healthcare system [3]. As such, it is the basis for referrals to secondary and tertiary level care.

At the next level, within *secondary care*, problems are handled that require more specialized clinical expertise [2] (e.g. a patient with acute renal failure). In comparison to primary care, services are provided by physicians and other health professionals who generally do not have first contact with patients. Moreover, secondary care is usually short-term, involving sporadic consultation from a specialist to provide expert opinion and/or surgical or other advanced interventions that primary care physicians (PCPs) are not equipped to perform [4]. Secondary care thus includes hospitalization, routine surgery, specialty consultation, and rehabilitation [4]. Note that secondary care is not necessarily only provided within a hospital. Many professionals work outside hospitals such as physiotherapists or psychiatrists.

Finally, *tertiary care* involves the management of rare and complex disorders [2]. This care is usually provided for inpatients and on referral from a primary or secondary care medical professional. Examples of tertiary care are trauma care, burn treatment, neonatal intensive care, tissue transplants, and open heart surgery. Typically, tertiary care is institution-based, highly specialized, and technology-driven [2]. Much of this kind of care is provided in large teaching hospitals, especially university-affiliated teaching hospitals [2].

Within [5], *emergency care* is considered as another level of care. This kind of care is provided by emergency medicine professionals. Their mission is to evaluate, manage, treat, and prevent unexpected illness and injury. Emergency physicians provide rapid assessment and treatment of any patient with a medical emergency. In addition, they are responsible for the initial assessment and care of any medical condition that a patient believes requires urgent attention, and they provide medical care for individuals who lack access to other kinds of care. Commonly, three levels of care are distinguished within emergency care. First, there are *non-urgent* patients which typically require primary care. Second, there are *emergent* patients which have immediate life of limb threatening problems. Third, there are *urgent* patients which fall in between the two other levels of care [6]. Clearly, emergent patients require immediate treatment whereas for non-urgent this is not necessarily needed.

2.2 Classification of Healthcare Processes

From the discussion above it becomes clear that patients' care processes may differ substantially. For patients in the same homogeneous patient group the process execution may be comparable but in case of complex patients, the accompanying process

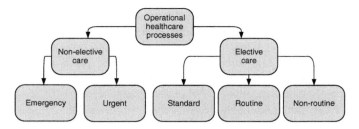

Fig. 2.1 Characterizing healthcare processes by outlining the main kinds of organizational healthcare processes

may exhibit many different execution outcomes. In order to come to a good understanding of the different characteristics of healthcare processes, Fig. 2.1 proposes a classification of the main kinds of healthcare processes that may coexist. Moreover, this classification is used to indicate on which kinds of processes the focus will be on in this book.

First of all, we only refer to care which is directly related to or provided for patients. In particular, the focus is on operational processes. These processes are concerned with the *logistics* of work processes. This involves the medical steps that need to be done together with the necessary preparations for these steps (e.g. the making of an appointment and the reservation of a room). As such we do not look into the process of individual decisions that are made by medical professionals with regard to diagnosis and treatments of patients. Also, for the activities within a process we do not look into the medical interpretation of them. Although these activities are included in a process mining analysis as individual events, we do not consider the results of these activities (e.g. the outcome of a blood test or X-ray) or any interpretation associated. In other words: *we focus on the orchestration and management of the care processes* rather than individual activities.

Given the above mentioned focus, in Fig. 2.1, operational processes are further subdivided into two main classes. *Elective care* relates to care for which it is medically sound to postpone treatment for days or weeks [7]. Conversely, *non-elective care* represents patient for whom medical treatment is unexpected and needs to be planned on short notice [7].

Elective care can range from processes that are completely standardized till processes for which a huge amount of variation exists. According to Lillrank et al. [8], a further division can be made into three subclasses. First, for *standard* processes a standardized treatment path exists which defines the different activities in the process and their timing. Given targets should be achieved if a treatment path is meticulously followed. Second, for *routine* processes, the overall outcome of the process is usually known. However, different process paths may be followed during treatment. Finally, within *non-routine* processes, the physician proceeds in a step-by-step way, checking the patient's reaction to an individual treatment and deciding about the steps to be taken next [9, 10]. Often, the decision about the next steps to be taken is not made by just one physician. When complex care needs to be delivered, cooperation between various physicians across different medical specialties and departments is needed to decide on and execute parts of the individual patient's care plan.

Finally, non-elective care can be further subdivided into two classes being emergency care and urgent care. *Emergency care* has to be performed immediately. In contrast, *urgent care* can be postponed for a short time (i.e. multiple days). The non-urgent patients mentioned earlier for emergency care [5] are considered to be elective care rather than non-elective care.

Considering the classification presented in Fig. 2.1 it is clear that many challenges exist related to the application of process mining on healthcare processes. For some processes, the discovered model may be relatively simple (standard care, routine care, and urgent care) whereas for other processes, the discovered process is much more spaghetti-like (emergency care and non-routine care). Furthermore, although processes may be standardized and homogeneous patient groups exist, still some variation may exist within a process. This relates to inter-physician variation and inter-practice variation within hospitals. With process mining such variations become visible.

2.3 Four Types of Questions

As mentioned in the introduction we distinguish four types of data science questions. After characterizing the different types of healthcare processes, we provide some example questions for each of the four categories.

- *What happened?*

    - What is the typical treatment of patients having acute myeloid leukemia?
    - How and when are patients transferred to an academic hospital?
    - What is the typical working day of a surgeon?
    - How is the new telehealth system used?

- *Why did it happen?*

    - What caused the unusual amount of incidents in the department?
    - Why was the service level agreement not reached?
    - Why did people stop using the telehealth system?
    - What caused the long waiting list?

- *What will happen?*

    - When will this patient be dismissed?
    - Is this patient likely to deviate from the normal treatment plan?
    - How many beds are needed tomorrow?
    - Is it possible to handle these five new cases in time?

- *What is the best that can happen?*
  - Which check should be done first to reduce flow time?
  - How many physicians are needed to reduce the waiting list by 50 %?
  - Does it help to do these tests concurrently?
  - How to redistribute the workload over the three surgeons?

As we will see in the remainder, such questions can be answered using process mining. In the next chapter an introduction to process mining is given. Chapter 4, introduces the healthcare reference model. Based on this reference model, Chap. 5 illustrates the array of analysis possibilities provided by process mining.

References

1. A. Rebuge and D.R. Ferreira. Business Process Analysis in Healthcare Environments: A Methodology Based on Process Mining. *Information Systems*, 37(2), 2012
2. K. Grumbach and T. Bodenheimer. The Organization of Health Care. *The Journal of the American Medical Association*, 273(2):160–167, 1995
3. "World Health Organization". A Glossary of Terms for Community Health Care and Services for Older Persons. WHO Centre for Health Development: Ageing and Health Technical Report 5, "WHO", 2004
4. L. Shi. The Impact of Primary Care: A Focused Review. *Scientifica*, 2012:22, 2012
5. B. Starfield. Is Primary Care Essential? *The Lancet*, 344:1129–1133, 1994
6. S.M. Schneider, G.C. Hamilton, P. Moyer, and J.S. Stapczynski. Definition of Emergency Medicine. *Academic Emergency Medicine*, 5(4):348–351, 1998
7. D. Gupta and B. Denton. Appointment Scheduling in Health Care: Challenges and Opportunities. *IIE Transactions*, 40(9):800–819, 2008
8. P. Lillrank and M. Liukko. Standard, Routine and Non-Routine Processes in Health Care. *International Journal of Health Care Quality Assurance*, 17(1):39–46, 2004
9. G de Vries, J W M Bertrand, and J M H Vissers. Design Requirements for Health Care Production Control Systems. *Production Planning & Control*, 10(6):559–569, 1999
10. J. Vissers and R. Beech. Chain Logistics: Analysis of Care Chains. In J. Vissers and R. Beech, editors, *Health Operations Management: Patient Flow Logistics in Health Care*, Routledge Health Management Series, pages 70–83. Routledge, 2005

Chapter 3
Process Mining

Abstract Process mining bridges the gap between traditional model-based process analysis (e.g., simulation and other business process management techniques) and data-centric analysis techniques such as machine learning and data mining. Process mining seeks the confrontation between event data (i.e., observed behavior) and process models (hand-made or discovered automatically). This technology has become available only recently, but is mature enough to be applied to care processes of any type and of any complexity. The process-mining spectrum is broad and includes techniques for process discovery, conformance checking, prediction, and bottleneck analysis. Traditional data-mining approaches are not process-centric. Input for data mining is typically a set of records and the output is a decision tree, a collection of clusters, or frequent patterns. Process mining starts from events and the output is related to an end-to-end process model. Data mining tools can be used to support particular decisions in a larger process. However, they cannot be used for process discovery, conformance checking, and other forms of process analysis. Therefore, process mining is needed to improve compliance and performance in hospitals in a systematic manner.

Keywords Process discovery · Conformance checking · Process mining · Event logs · Healthcare · Business process management

Given an event log, the goal of process mining is to extract process knowledge (e.g. process models) in order to discover, monitor, and improve real processes [1]. These event logs may originate from a wide range of systems. Examples of these systems are Business Process Management (BPM) systems (e.g. *BPM|One*, *Filenet*), ERP systems (e.g. *Microsoft Dynamics NAV* and *SAP*), Product Data Management (PDM) systems (e.g. *Windchill*), and Hospital Information Systems (e.g. *i.s.h.med*, *iSOFT*, *ChipSoft*, *McKesson*, and *Epic*). In later chapters we will focus on the typical event data found in the latter class of systems. However, first we provide a brief overview of process mining.

© The Author(s) 2015
R.S. Mans et al., *Process Mining in Healthcare*,
SpringerBriefs in Business Process Management, DOI 10.1007/978-3-319-16071-9_3

3.1 Event Data and Process Models

Within an event log certain information needs to be present in order to apply process mining. Figure 3.1 depicts the typical information that needs to be available in terms of a UML class diagram [2]. Furthermore, the relation between an event log and a process model is visualized. Three levels are identified: model level, instance level, and event level. The model level and the event level typically *exist independent of one another*; people make process models without relating to (raw) data in the information system and processes generate data while being unaware of the process models that may exist.

The instance level consists of *cases* and *activity instances*. These connect *processes* and *activities* in the model to *events* in the log. There are several important relationships between these five concepts together with their cardinalities. At the model level, a process may have an arbitrary number of activities, but each activity belongs to precisely one process (cardinality 1 . . *). An event log contains information about a single process. Such a process may consist of multiple cases but each every case only belongs to precisely one process (cardinality 1 . . *). Furthermore, each event in the log belongs to a single case (cardinality 1 . . *). Events are related to activities. In particular, every event corresponds to one activity instance (cardinality 1 . . *) whereas each activity instance refers to precisely one activity (cardinality 1 . . *).

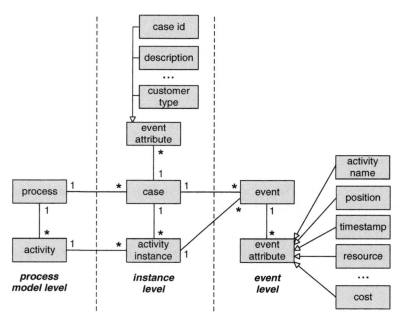

Fig. 3.1 The typical information that needs to be present in an event log. Additionally, the relation between a process model and a event log is depicted

Note that multiple activity instances may exist for one activity and that for the same activity instance there may be multiple events. Furthermore, every activity instance belongs to precisely one case (cardinality 1 . . *).

For cases and events additional information may exist. This information is contained in attributes (cardinality 1 . . *). Each attribute consists of a name and a value (e.g. "(resource, Ferdinand)"). For an event, two attributes deserve some special attention. In order to discover causal dependencies in process models, events need to be ordered. This requirement is satisfied if all events have a *timestamp* representing the time at which the event occurred. In case this information is not available, a *position* attribute is needed which specifies the index of an event in a case. Note that timestamp information can be used for calculating performance properties of the process. The "resource" attribute (performer of the event) and the "cost" attribute (cost of the activity) can be used for inferring additional process knowledge.

An example log is shown in Fig. 3.2a. The table contains 16 events for 3 cases. For example, for the case with id "1", subsequently the activities "Fist Visit", "Surgery", "Second Visit", "Radiotherapy", "Chemotherapy" and "Evaluate" have been performed. Here, the "Fist Visit" event has id "4798669", is performed by "Pete" at "02/06/2014 14:00:00", and has cost "150".

Obliviously, process mining is related to data mining, machine learning and Business Intelligence (BI). These also aim at knowledge discovery, performance measurement, and prediction [3]. However, process mining is process-centric, an aspect largely ignored by mainstream data mining, machine learning and BI techniques. Process mining starts with making unknown (or only partially known) processes explicit in terms of end-to-end process models (not just patterns).

Process mining is also closely related to *Business Process Management* (BPM). Figure 3.3 shows a variant of the classical BPM lifecycle. In the *(re)design phase*, a process model is designed. This model is transformed into a running system in the *implementation/configuration phase*. If the model is already in executable form and a WFM or BPM system is already running, this phase may be very short. However, if the model is informal and needs to be hardcoded in conventional software, this phase may take substantial time. After the system supports the designed processes, the *run & adjust phase* starts. In this phase, the processes are enacted and adjusted when needed. In the run & adjust phase, the process is not redesigned and no new software is created; only predefined controls are used to adapt or reconfigure the process.

Next to the BPM lifecycle, Fig. 3.3 also shows the two main types of analysis: *model-based analysis* and *data-based analysis*. While the system is running, event data are collected. These data can be used to analyze running processes, e.g., discover bottlenecks, waste, and deviations. This is input for the redesign phase. During this phase process models can be used for analysis. For example, simulation is used for what-if analysis or the correctness of a new design is verified using model checking. In recent years the focus in BPM shifted from purely model-based analysis to data-based analysis, thus explaining the growing interest in process mining.

(a)

Case id	Event id	Properties			
		Timestamp	Activity	Resource	Cost
1	4798669	02/06/2014 14:00	First Visit	Pete	150
	4798670	07/06/2014 11:00	Surgery	Rose	55
	4798677	09/06/2014 17:00	Second Visit	Pete	150
	4798679	12/06/2014 12:15	Radiotherapy	Alfred	200
	4798680	14/06/2014 12:15	Chemotherapy	Michael	300
	4798685	17/06/2014 10:00	Evaluate	Pete	175
2	7777171	05/06/2014 09:15	First Visit	John	120
	7777195	13/06/2014 14:30	Surgery	Nick	610
	7777189	15/06/2014 15:45	Second Visit	John	120
	7777179	27/06/2014 11:45	Chemotherapy	Michael	300
	7777195	29/06/2014 14:30	Radiotherapy	Alfred	200
	7777185	08/07/2014 08:15	Evaluate	Pete	180
3	7932191	12/06/2014 14:45	First Visit	John	120
	7932192	23/06/2014 11:00	Surgery	Rose	55
	7932196	25/06/2014 08:00	Second Visit	John	120
	7932192	01/07/2014 16:00	Radiotherapy	Alfred	200
	7932193	07/07/2014 17:30	Chemotherapy	Michael	300
	7932196	21/07/2014 08:00	Evaluate	John	185

(b)

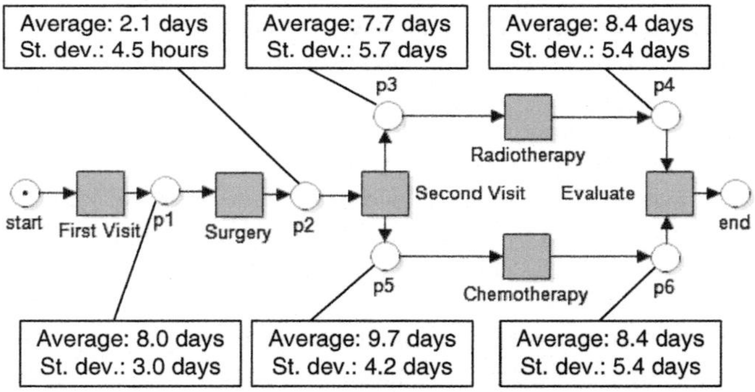

Fig. 3.2 Example of an event log together with discovered process knowledge. **a** A fragment of an event log: each line corresponds to an event. **b** Discovered Petri net for the event log fragment. Additionally, for the places some statistics are shown concerning the time spent in the places

Figure 3.4 again shows that process mining is the missing link between analysis techniques that focus on process models without considering the actual event data and classical data-oriented analysis with no attention to end-to-end processes. The figure also shows that process mining can be used to answer both *compliance-related* (e.g., where and why do physicians deviate?) and *performance-related* (e.g., where are the main bottlenecks and how to remove them?) *questions*.

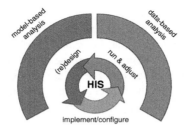

Fig. 3.3 The BPM lifecyle and the role of data-based analysis versus model-based analysis

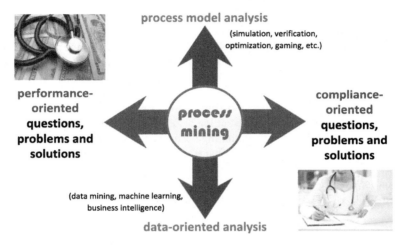

Fig. 3.4 Process mining aims to answer performance-related and compliance-related questions

3.2 Three Types of Process Mining

In general, three main types of process mining can be distinguished (see Fig. 3.5).
Discovery: Here the focus is on inferring process models (e.g. a Petri net or a BPMN model) that are able to describe the observed behavior. For example, the inferred model may describe the typical steps that are taken within a process.

Figure 3.2b shows a Petri net that is discovered for the event log of Fig. 3.2a. As can be seen for all cases, the process starts with a "First Visit". Next, a "Surgery" and the "Second visit" is performed. After that both "Radiotherapy" and "Chemotherapy" are performed. Note that these two activities may be performed in any order. Finally, an evaluation (task "Evaluate") is taking place. Note that also models describing the organizational or data perspectives may be discovered.

Conformance: for a given model it is checked whether it conforms to observed behavior in the event log. In case there are deviations between the model and the event log these are identified such that they can be further analyzed (e.g. activities in the model that cannot be found in the event log or the other way around).

For example, for the traces shown in Fig. 3.2a it can be seen that all their events can be successfully replayed in the model of Fig. 3.2b. However, consider the trace with events "First visit", "Surgery", "Second visit", "Radiotherapy" and "Evaluate". When replaying this trace it is found that the "Chemotherapy" event is missing. Next, for the trace with events "First visit", "Surgery", "Second Visit", "Chemotherapy", "Lab test", "Radiotherapy", and "Evaluate" it can be seen that an lab test is done in between the "Second visit" and "Evaluate" activities.

Enhancement: information extracted from the log is projected onto the model. Note that here it is assumed that already a model exists (either discovered or made by hand). Using the seminal notion of alignments, trace in the log can be connected to paths in the model (even in case of deviations). Alignments can be used to "repair" a process model, i.e., the model is enhanced by making it closer to reality, but still retaining as much as possible from the original model. Alignments can also be used to enrich the model with additional perspectives (times, costs, risks, decisions, resource usage, etc.). For example, in the example event log also timestamp information is found for the events. This can be used for calculating performance information concerning the discovered process shown in Fig. 3.2. That is, for each place in the model the average time that is spent by a token in that place is indicated. Additionally, the standard deviation is given. For example, the average time in between a "Surgery" and the "Second Visit" is 2.1 days (standard deviation: 4.5 h).

Fig. 3.5 Three types of process mining: (1) Discovery, (2) Conformance, and (3) Extension

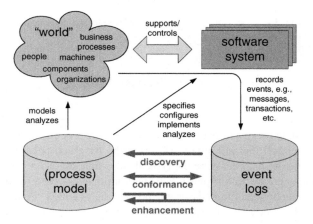

3.3 The Process Mining Spectrum

Thus far we identified three main types of process mining: *discovery*, *conformance*, and *enhancement*. However, this does not reflect the broadness of the process mining spectrum. Orthogonal to there three types of process mining are perspectives such as the *control-flow perspective* ("How?"), the *organizational perspective* ("Who?"), and the *case/data perspective* ("What?"). Moreover, analysis can be done *online* or *off-line*.

Figure 3.6 (taken from [1]) shows the so-called refined process mining framework. Data in event logs are partitioned into "*pre mortem*" and "*post mortem*" *event data*. "Post mortem" event data refer to information about cases that have completed, i.e., these data can be used for process improvement and auditing, but not for influencing the cases they refer to. "Pre mortem" event data refer to cases that have not yet completed. If a case is still running, i.e., the case is still "alive" (pre mortem), then it may be possible that information in the event log about this case (i.e., current data)

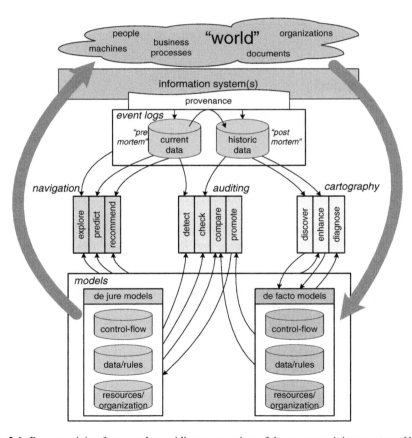

Fig. 3.6 Process mining framework providing an overview of the process mining spectrum [1]

can be exploited to ensure the correct or efficient handling of this case. The refined process mining framework also distinguishes between two types of models: "*de jure models*" and "*de facto models*". *A de jure model is normative*, i.e., it specifies how things should be done or handled. For example, a process model used to configure a BPM system is normative and forces people to work in a particular way. *A de facto model is descriptive* and its goal is not to steer or control reality. Instead, de facto models aim to capture reality adequately.

By combining the different types of event data ("pre mortem" or "post mortem"), the different types of perspectives (control-flow, organizational, data, costs, etc.), and the different types of models ("de jure" and "de facto models") the broadness of the field becomes obvious. Figure 3.6 lists ten process-mining related activities.

More and more organizations are adopting process mining as a means to improve operational performance and conformance. For example, the web site of the IEEE Task Force on Process Mining[1] which lists over 15 successful case studies in industry. Process mining has also been applied in several Dutch hospitals (Isala Hospital Zwolle, Maastricht University Medical Center, Academic Medical Center Amsterdam, Catharina Hospital Eindhoven, Mental Healthcare Institute Eindhoven, Albert Schweitzer Hospital Dordrecht, etc.).

3.4 Tool Support

The *ProM* framework[2] is the de facto standard for process mining aiming to cover the whole spectrum shown in Fig. 3.6 [1, 4]. ProM is a "plug-able" environment for process mining using MXML, SA-MXML, or XES as input format. Import tools like ProMimport and XESame can be used to convert data from various sources into event logs. Moreover, tools like Disco and ProM can also read CSV files and interpret these as event logs. ProM provides hundreds of plug-ins supporting the ten process mining related activities shown in Fig. 3.6.

The uptake of process mining is not only illustrated by the growing number of papers and plug-ins of the open source tool *ProM*, there are also a growing number of commercial analysis tools providing process mining capabilities, cf. *Disco* (Fluxicon), *Perceptive Process Mining* (Perceptive Software, before Futura Reflect and BPMone by Pallas Athena), *ARIS Process Performance Manager* (Software AG), *Celonis Process Mining* (Celonis GmbH), *ProcessAnalyzer* (QPR), *Interstage Process Discovery* (Fujitsu), *Discovery Analyst* (StereoLOGIC), and *XMAnalyzer* (XMPro). Many of the ideas developed in the context of ProM have been embedded in these commercial tools.

Mainstream BI software like IBM Cognos Business Intelligence (IBM), Oracle Business Intelligence (Oracle), SAP BusinessObjects (SAP), WebFOCUS (Information Builders), MS SQL Server (Microsoft), MicroStrategy (MicroStrategy),

---

[1] www.win.tue.nl/ieeetfpm/doku.php?id=shared:process_mining_case_studies.

[2] www.processmining.org.

NovaView (Panorama Software), QlikView (QlikTech), SAS Enterprise Business
Intelligence (SAS), TIBCO Spotfire Analytics (TIBCO), Jaspersoft (Jaspersoft), and
Pentaho BI Suite (Pentaho) are *not* process oriented and therefore less suitable for
answering process mining questions. Similar comments can be made about data mining tools. Although both process mining and data mining start from data, data mining
techniques are typically not process-centric and do not focus on event data. For data
mining techniques the rows (instances) and columns (variables) can mean anything.
For process mining techniques, we assume event data where events refer to process
instances and activities. Moreover, the events are ordered and we are interested in
end-to-end processes rather than local patterns. End-to-end process models and con-
currency are essential for process mining. Moreover, topics such as process discovery,
conformance checking, and bottleneck analysis are not addressed by traditional data
mining techniques and tools (Fig. 3.7).

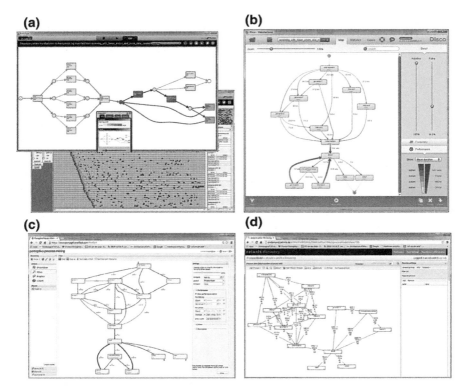

Fig. 3.7 Four screenshots of different tools analyzing the same event log: **a** *ProM* (open source),
b *Disco* (Fluxicon), **c** *Perceptive Process Mining* (Perceptive Software), and **d** *Celonis Process
Mining* (Celonis GmbH)

Data mining (in the narrow sense) and process mining are complementary approaches that can strengthen each other. Process models (once discovered and aligned with the event log) provide the basis for valuable data mining questions. This is illustrated by *RapidProM* (the RapidMiner ProM 6 Extension[3]). The relation between different types of analysis is discussed later in this *SpringerBrief*.

References

1. W.M.P. van der Aalst. *Process Mining: Discovery Conformance and Enhancement of Business Processes*. Springer-Verlag, Berlin, 2011
2. Object Management Group. *OMG Unified Modeling Language, Version 2.0*. Object Management Group, 2005
3. D. Hand, H. Mannilla, and P. Smyth. *Principles of Data Mining*. MIT Press, Cambridge, MA, 2001
4. H.M.W. Verbeek, J.C.A.M. Buijs, B.F. van Dongen, and W.M.P. van der Aalst. XES, XESame, and ProM 6. In *Information Systems Evolution*, volume 72 of *Lecture Notes in Computer Science*, pages 60–75. Springer Verlag Berlin-Heidelberg, 2011

---

[3] www.rapidprom.org.

Chapter 4
Healthcare Reference Model

Abstract Data science projects in hospitals often fail because of data-related problems. The data are somewhere in the Hospital Information System (HIS), but the analyst cannot find it or extraction is too costly. Therefore, a healthcare reference model was developed. The goal is to locate event data easily and to support data extraction. Moreover, the analyst can use the model to ask the right questions. The healthcare reference model was developed based on an analysis of the available data in several Dutch hospitals. The reference model is described in terms of a UML class diagram. The model consists of 122 classes that provide a good overview of the key data relevant for process mining. It was validated by HIS professionals of the AMC, Catharina, and Isala hospitals.

Keywords Healthcare reference model · Hospital information systems · Process mining · Healthcare · Event data · UML class diagram

In this section, we discuss the *healthcare reference model* outlining all the different classes of data that can be available for process mining together with the associated relationships between these classes of data. Figure 4.1 illustrates the role of this reference model. Without such a model it is difficult to reason about questions that may or may not be answered using process mining. Often stakeholders are not aware of the wealth of data in their own systems. Moreover, data extraction is done through "trial and error" rather than a demand-driven approach. Often data are extracted without having a question in mind. Of course there is nothing wrong with exploring the data available. However, data extraction is often done by people not analyzing the data. Therefore, our healthcare reference model is instrumental in locating the data needed and facilitating the actual extraction.

In the healthcare reference model, we focus on the classes that relate to the classification provided in Fig. 2.1. The reference model is described in terms of a UML class diagram [1]. Before discussing the reference model, we first describe the approach for building the model in Sect. 4.1. Second, the model itself is described in Sect. 4.2. Finally, in Sect. 4.3 we elaborate on the validation of the model.

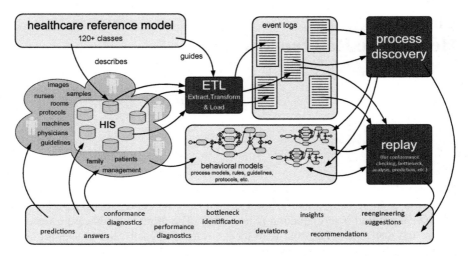

Fig. 4.1 The healthcare reference model is used as a starting point for locating the data and extracting event logs

4.1 Development Approach

In order to build the *healthcare reference model* the following two-step approach was used. First, we developed an initial version of the healthcare reference model by investigating an actual running implementation of a system within a hospital. More precisely, in the context of an existing collaboration between MUMC and TU/e we have investigated the *i.s.h.med* system of Siemens Healthcare[1] that is in use at the hospital. In this system, detailed information was available concerning the tables that are present and the content of these tables, i.e. the names of the columns in the tables. Also, it was possible to learn about the usage of the system in practice by interviewing people and by inspecting the system itself. Moreover, data from practice could be obtained by extracting data from multiple tables (see Chap. 5). Secondly, we validated the initial version of this reference model by investigating systems that were in use in other hospitals. That is, the reference model was discussed with several of their HIS professionals in order to identify missing data entities and to further revise the model. We had interviews with professionals of the AMC hospital in Amsterdam, the Netherlands,[2] the Catharina hospital in Eindhoven, the Netherlands,[3] and the Isala hospital in Zwolle, the Netherlands.[4] Moreover, we were able to investigate (some of) their systems.

---

[1] http://healthcare.siemens.com/hospital-it/clinical-information-systems/clinical-information-systems-ishmed.

[2] http://www.amc.nl.

[3] http://www.cze.nl.

[4] http://www.isala.nl.

We do not claim that the resulting version of the healthcare reference model is complete. However, we believe that by following the above mentioned approach the reference model represents, for a typical HIS, the key data elements that are related to process mining.

4.2 The Model

In total, the reference model consists of 122 classes. We use the following grouping:

- **General Patient and Case Data**: General information about patients and the cases that are executed for them. Here, a case refers to an illness for which a patient receives treatment.
- **Process Steps**: Information about all steps that are performed for patients and the refinement of steps into more fine-grained steps or events.
  - **Medication**: Drugs that are given to patients.
  - **Patient Transport**: The transportation of patients within the hospital.
  - **Radiology**: Radiology examinations that are performed for patients.
- **Document Data**: The medical data that are saved in the context of steps that are performed for patients.
- **Organization and Buildings**: The organizational and building related structure within the hospital.
- **Nursing Plans**: Plans for the care that is given by nurses to patients.
- **Pathways**: The definition of pathways.

Note that the first two groups ("general patient and case data" and "processes steps") relate to general information about patients and the process steps that have been performed for them. Subsequently, in the "patient transport", "medication", and "radiology" groups, we illustrate some more fine grained process information that can be found for the steps related to patient transport, radiology, and medication. The "document data" and "organization and buildings" groups define additional data that can be found for the performed services and patients in general, i.e. medical documentation and resources that are involved. Finally, in the "nursing plans" and "pathways" groups we elaborate on process knowledge that is stored about nursing plans and pathways. These groups provide guidelines about diagnosing and treating patients.

Below, each group is discussed in more detail. This is done by focusing on the classes that have been modeled for the group and the relationships between these classes. Moreover, several attributes are provided in order to illustrate the data in a class. Here, we particularly focus on these attributes that are important for process mining, i.e. names of steps, timestamps, resources, and case identifiers. The attributes that together uniquely identify each record in a class, i.e. the primary key, are indicated by the "+" character in front of them. Similarly, an attribute which is not a private key is illustrated by a "−" character.

4.2.1 General Patient and Case Data

For a patient, general information that is important for the entire treatment trajectory in the hospital is stored. The associated classes are shown in Fig. 4.2. For a patient (class patient) general information exists such as patient number, name, sex, birthdate, religion, and telephone number. Note that the patient number is a primary key in the patient class as indicated by the "+" character. As shown in Fig. 4.2, a patient may suffer from multiple health problems (class

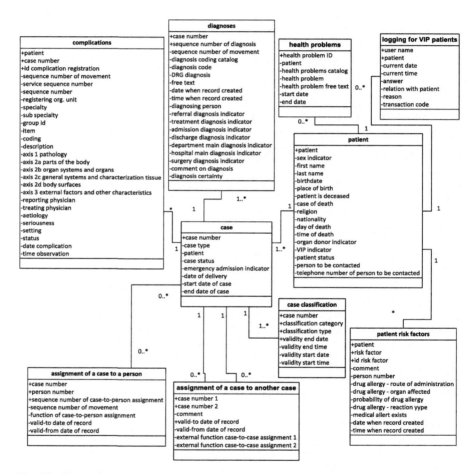

Fig. 4.2 Classes describing general information for patients and cases. A patient (patient class) may suffer from multiple health problems (class health problems) and multiple risk factors may apply (class patient risk factors). For a patient multiple (ongoing) cases may be recorded (case class). Furthermore, multiple kinds of information may be recorded for a case such as the complications that occurred (complications class) or the diagnoses (diagnoses) that have been determined

health problems for which the associated multiplicity is 0..*) and multiple risk factors may exist for a patient (class risk factors for which the associated multiplicity is 0..*). Also, if a patient is a Very Important Person (VIP) then all transactions that take place may need to be logged (class logging for VIP patients with associated multiplicity 0..*).

A patient may suffer from multiple illnesses. For each illness a separate case is created (class case for which the associated multiplicity is 0..*). Note that for a case it is saved on which day the case started and on which day it is completed. Related to a case, information is saved about complications that have been observed (class complications), diagnoses that have been identified (class diagnoses), the assignment of persons to a case (class assignment of a case to a person), and the classification categories which belong to a case (class case classification). Moreover, during treatment it may be desired to assign a case to another case (class assignment of a case to another case). For example, a complication might lead to assigning two cases to each other.

For several classes, timing information is recorded. Regarding the complications and diagnoses, the exact date and time is recorded on which respectively the complication occurred and the diagnosis was made. Furthermore, for a classification category of a case and an assignment of a case to a person it is specifically saved for which period it is valid, i.e. for each record the start and end date of its validity is recorded.

4.2.2 Process Steps

For a case, several steps can be performed. In Figs. 4.3, 4.4 and 4.5 it is visualized which information is stored about the process steps that have been performed. For these process steps we look at their timing and at which level of granularity they

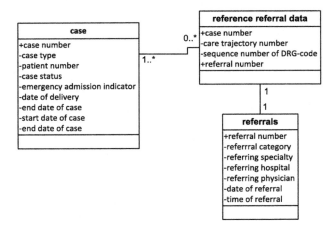

Fig. 4.3 Classes describing the referral of patients

are saved. In total 26 different classes are defined. Three groups of classes can be distinguished: (1) the referral of the patient to the hospital; (2) the different kinds of process steps that are recorded during diagnosis and treatment; and (3) the registration of orders and appointments.

4.2.2.1 Referral

In Fig. 4.3 the classes regarding the referral of patients are shown. For a referred patient it is recorded on which day the patient is referred (class `referrals`). Furthermore, additional information about the referral is recorded such as the referring hospital and the kind of referral (e.g. via the general practitioner, emergency, or self-referral). Also, a referral number is created which is important in order to link the patient to one or more cases (class `reference referral data` with associated multiplicity `1..*`).

4.2.2.2 Different Kinds of Process Steps

Figure 4.4 shows all classes which are related to the recording of process steps during the diagnosis and treatment of patients. At the coarsest level of granularity the cases of illness from which a patient suffers (class `cases`) are stored. A case may consist of multiple so-called movements (class `movements for case` with associated multiplicity `1..*`). A movement can be seen as an encounter between a patient and a healthcare provider which spans a period of time. Furthermore, the length and detail of a movement may vary according to local procedures, conventions, and data capturing standards. A movement can be seen as a step which is defined at a coarse level of granularity. Examples are a stay at the nursing ward, a visit to the outpatient clinic, or a surgical intervention.

As a part of a movement, multiple services may be delivered to a patient (class `services performed` with associated multiplicity `0..*`). Similar to a movement, a service spans a period of time but its duration is typically shorter than the duration of a movement. Also, its level of detail is more fine-grained and refers to a concrete piece-of-work that is performed by a person. For example, a physician may perform multiple services during a visit of a patient to an outpatient clinic (which is a movement), such as an echography and an intake. As can be seen in Fig. 4.4, a service can be further specialized into two kinds of services. Medical services (class `medical service`) relate to diagnostic and therapeutic services which are performed for patients (e.g. an X-ray or the removal of a tumor) and non-medical services (class `non-medical service`) relate to the coordination of healthcare professionals and the support of a patient and his relatives (e.g. informing the family about the status of a patient). For services, the involvement of each person is recorded including the period during which each person was involved (class `involved staff members`). Because a service refers to a concrete piece of a work, many additional attributes may exist for a specific service itself.

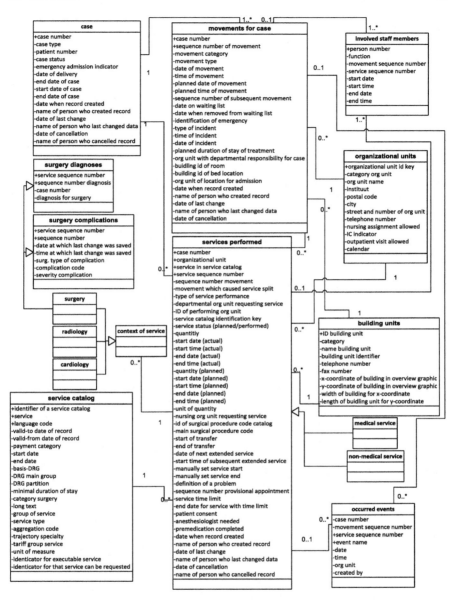

Fig. 4.4 Classes describing the process steps that are performed and which may reside at different levels of granularity. That is, for a case (`case` class) multiple movements may be recorded (class `movements`). Similarly, one or more services may have been performed as part of a movement (`services performed`). As part of a service or movement multiple events may have occurred (`occurred events`). A service can be a medical service (class `medical service`) or a non-medical service (`non-medical service` class)

This is illustrated by the attributes in the class `service catalog`. For example, its type, costs, minimal duration, and by which discipline it may be performed is stored. Furthermore, some specific context attributes may exist (class `context of service`) which may be different for medical disciplines (classes `surgery`, `radiology`, and `cardiology`). For example, in the context of a surgery it is recorded which specific diagnoses are relevant (class `surgery diagnoses`) and which complications occurred (class `surgery complications`).

For a service or a movement even more fine-grained information may exist. This is illustrated by the `occurred events` class which refers to events that have occurred as part of a service or a movement. For example, a surgery "movement" includes several events such as the request of transporting the patient to the surgical department, the arrival of the patient in the holding area, the arrival of the patient in the operating room, the start of the induction,[5] the departure from the operation room, and the arrival in the recovery room.

Note that for each case, movement, and service information exists about the person who created, modified, and canceled a record together with its timing. Furthermore, each movement and service includes information about which organizational unit requested it and the organizational unit for which it has been performed.

4.2.2.3 Orders and Appointments

Figure 4.5 relates to orders and appointments that are created for patients and the associated relationships. As already indicated earlier, a movement spans a period of time during which multiple services can be performed. An appointment can only be made for a movement (class `appointments` with associated multiplicity $1..1$). An appointment can be booked into the calendar of one or more resources (e.g. a physician (class `involved staff members`), a room) and has a start and end date and time. Furthermore, information can be kept about the date when the patient was last notified and the date and time of the appointment at that time. Note that it is not required that for each movement an appointment exists.

The booking of one or more appointments for a patient can be triggered via a clinical order (class `clinical order` with associated multiplicity $0..*$). This may involve putting the patient on a waiting list. As part of the latter, it is recorded at which time the patient is put on the waiting list. Also, timing information is recorded describing if and when a patient was temporarily absent from the waiting list. An order may consist of multiple order items (class `item of clinical order` with associated multiplicity $0..*$). For each order item an appointment may be created and linked to the corresponding movement (e.g. for a surgery it is needed to make an appointment for the preoperative assessment, the surgical intervention itself, and the admission to the nursing ward). For an order item some aspects can be filled in which are important for the appointment to be made (e.g. the performing organizational

---

[5] Induction is an anesthesiological term for the administration of a drug or combination of drugs at the beginning of an anesthetic that results in a state of general anesthesia.

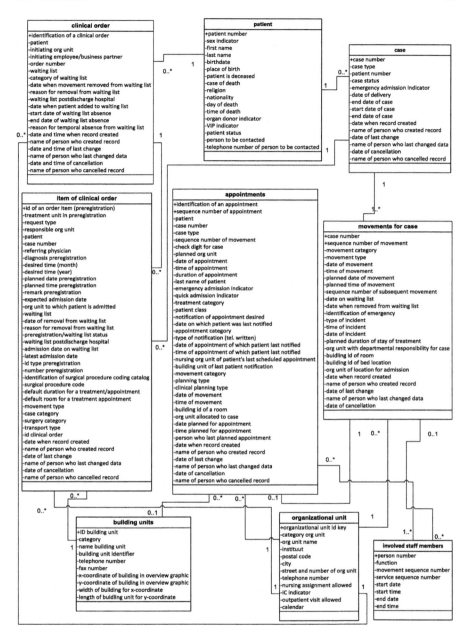

Fig. 4.5 Classes related to orders and appointments that are made for patients. Only for a movement an appointment can be made (`appointments` class). An appointment may be booked as part of an item of a clinical order (`item of clinical order` class). Note that an order item is part of a clinical order (`clinical order` class)

unit, the referring physician, the default duration and room of the appointment, and the desired time of the appointment). Note that it is not required that for each appointment an order item exists (e.g. an appointment for a visit to the outpatient clinic). Also, an order does not always need to refer to an appointment (e.g. an order may also be created for a medication that needs to be given). For appointments, clinical orders, and order items, information may be kept about the requesting and performing organizational unit and the involved building unit. Furthermore, also here, information exists about the person who created, modified, and canceled a record together with its timing.

4.2.3 Medication

Many patients receive medication during their stay in the hospital. The classes that are related to the provision of medication are given in Fig. 4.6. For the majority of drugs that are given first an order is created (class `drug order`). Drugs may be given on an incidental basis if needed. Note that the drug order can either be linked to a case (the attached multiplicity is `0..*`) or a patient in case the medication is relevant for multiple cases (the attached multiplicity is `0..*`). Within an order, the ordering organizational unit and responsible employee is indicated. Furthermore, the validity of the drug order, i.e. the period of time in which the drugs may be given, and its number of repeats can be indicated. A drug order may consist of multiple lines (class `drug order line`). Therefore, the multiplicity attached to the `drug` class is `1..*`. Note that for each drug some basic information exists such as the manufacturer, its validity, and the way it needs to be administered (class `drug formulary`). For a drug order that needs to be given per infusion, some details are given about the dosage quantities (class `dosage quantities infusions`).

Once it is decided that a drug is needed, the drug itself needs to be administered (class `drug event`). As for one order, the drug may need to be administered multiple times the multiplicity attached to the `drug event` class is `1..*`. Amongst others, for the administration of a drug, it is important that the planned start date and time, the cycle start date and time, the actual administration date and time, the planned dosage, and the person who administered the drug are given. Furthermore, it is indicated for each drug event which drugs are administered (class `drug event - drug assignment`). Closely related to the administration of a drug is that it may need to be prepared (class `preparation documentation of event` with associated multiplicity `0..1`). Here, it is saved who prepared the drug. As a next step, some preparation steps may be needed before the drug is actually given (class `preparation for administration documentation of event`). Finally, with regard to the administration (class `event administration event` with associated multiplicity `1`) the real administration date and time and the real quantity that is administered is saved.

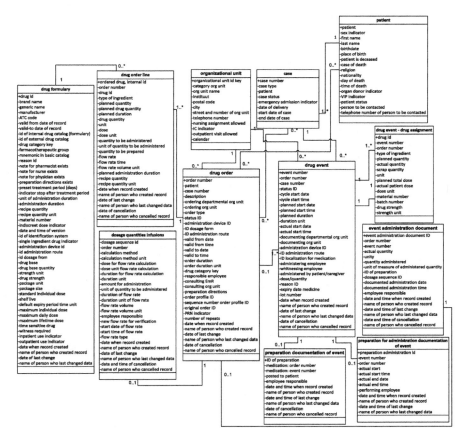

Fig. 4.6 The provision of medication to patients. As a first step, a drug order needs to be created (`drug order` class). Afterwards, the drug may be provided multiple times (`drug event` class). For each provided drug, its preparation is recorded (`preparation documentation of event` class) and the person who administered the drug (`event administration document` class)

4.2.4 Patient Transport

Some patients need to be transported within the hospital. Figure 4.7 shows the classes that are involved around the transport of patients. In order for a transport to take place, a transport order needs to be created (class `transport order`). A transport order may have various attributes, e.g. the transporter needs to be defined, the details of the appointment and the room from which the patient needs to be picked-up, and the details of the appointment and the room to which the patient needs to be transported need to be given. Note that information about the person who created, modified, and canceled a record together with its timing are logged.

Fig. 4.7 The transportation of patients within the hospital. Each transport order (`transport order` class) defines the appointment from which the patient needs to be picked-up and the appointment to which the patient needs to be transported

4.2.5 Radiology

For radiological examinations, typically a well defined workflow exists. The associated classes are shown in Fig. 4.8. In case a radiological examination is requested, a radiology service exists. To this service, medical documentation is attached. Therefore, the `link for assignment of documents` class of Fig. 4.9 is repeated in Fig. 4.8 in order to link medical documentation to the radiology service. In this documentation is kept which procedure is requested and its priority (class `radiological service / examination`). This is needed for creating the corresponding worklist (class `radiology worklist`) together with additional attributes (class `radiological worklist for optional attributes`). Note that a procedure is the radiological equivalent of a medical

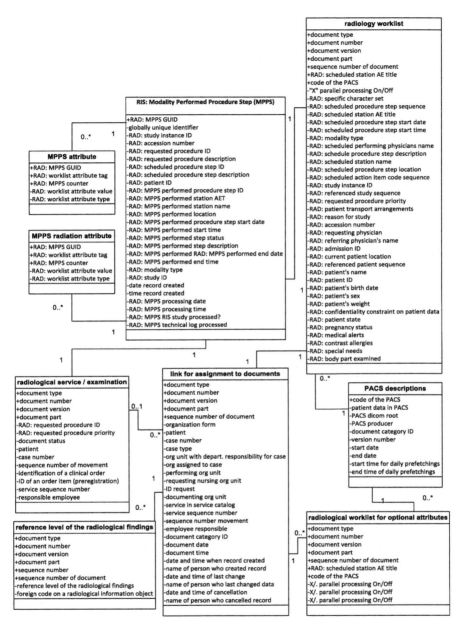

Fig. 4.8 The radiological examinations for patients. As part of such an examination multiple procedures may take place (`radiological service / examination` class) which all appear in the specific worklist that is created for the patient (`radiology worklist` class). Moreover, each procedure is performed on a modality (`RIS: Modality Performed Procedure Step (MPPS)` class)

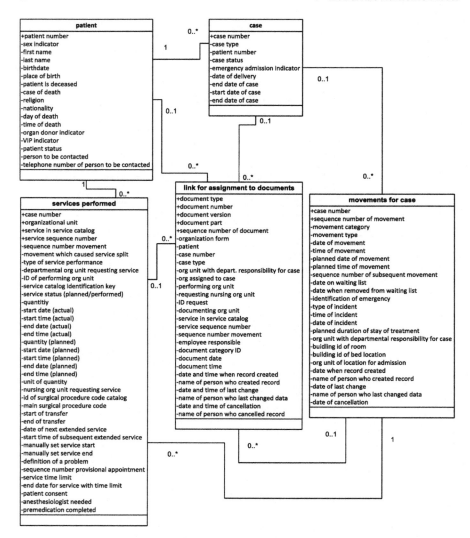

Fig. 4.9 Linkage of medical documents to patients, cases, movements, and performed services. For each of them, multiple links may exist (`link for assignment to documents` class)

service. In the worklist, the entire planning of the required procedure can be found (e.g. the scheduled procedure step, the start date and time of the procedure step, the station at which the procedure is going to take place, and the scheduled physician who will perform the procedure) and the arrangement of the patient transport if needed. In order to be able to perform the procedure properly, general information about the patient is kept. Note that also an *accession number* is kept. This is a well-known number in radiology. It represents a single patient encounter to a specific radiological procedure. Therefore, this number is also used for the procedure step that is performed on a modality (class RIS: Modality Performed Procedure Step (MPPS)). For each procedure, its actual performed procedure step, timing, processing time, and the station on which the procedure is performed is stored. Additionally, specific attributes (class MPPS attribute with associated multiplicity 0..*) or radiation related attributes may need to be saved (class MPPS radiation attribute with associated multiplicity 0..*). Finally, the entire examination is completed by reporting the findings (class reference level of the radiological findings). This consists of the storage of the obtained images in the Picture Archiving and Communication System (PACS).

4.2.6 Document Data

Related to the entire treatment trajectory of a patient many medical documents are created. The information contained in these documents may either be structured, unstructured, or both. As shown in Fig. 4.9, for patients, cases of illness, movements, and services performed, a link with medical documentation is possible (class link for assignments to documents). For all four, multiple links may exist as indicated by the multiplicity 0..*. However, medical documentation is not obligatory for each of them (multiplicity 0..1).

In the entire hospital there are many kinds of documents each containing specific information. Nevertheless, as shown in Figs. 4.10, 4.11 and 4.12, still some commonalities exist for them. First of all, multiple documents may be attached to each document link (class header document with associated multiplicity 1..*). In this way, it can be indicated that multiple documents may exist for a patient, cases of illness, movements, and services.

Figure 4.10 outlines the main classes that can be distinguished with regard to medical documentation. For some of the classes, a more detailed classification is provided in Figs. 4.11 and 4.12. According to Fig. 4.10, medical documentation can be divided into documentation that is created by a physician (physician EPR), by a nurse (nursing EPR), and documentation that is provided by a allied health professional (allied health profession EPR), such as a physiotherapist (physiotherapy) and a dietician (dietician).[6]

In Fig. 4.11 more details are provided regarding documentation created by a nurse. The documents created by a nurse are typically centered around the clinical admission of a patient. A distinction can be made into documents that relate to activities that are performed by a nurse (class nursing activity log document) and documents that relate to outcomes of the nursing care that is provided (class nursing care outcomes document). Examples of nursing care outcomes documents are the outcomes of the anamnesis done at the start of the clinical admission (class nursing EPR: nursing anamnesis) and the

---

[6] Note that EPR is an abbreviation for Electronic Patient Record.

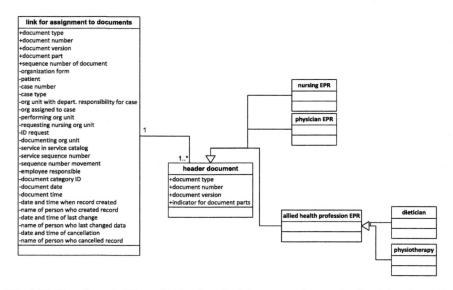

Fig. 4.10 Overview of different kinds of medical documents that can be found in a hospital. There are specific documents that are created by a nurse (`nursing EPR` class), by a physician (`physician EPR` class), and that are created by a allied health professional (`allied health profession EPR` class)

evaluation of pain where a patient suffers from (`nursing EPR: anamnesis pain evaluation`). Examples of activity log documents are the aftercare that is provided to a patient via telephone (class `aftercare via telephone`) and checklists that are filled in (class `checklist`). Checklists are nowadays becoming more popular as it helps ensuring that no step will be forgotten. Moreover, it helps in increasing patient safety and patient outcomes [2]. An example of a checklist is a discharge checklist which is filled in 48 h after admission (class `discharge checklist 48 h after admission`).

For documentation created by physicians, we make a distinction between a generic document (class `basic document generic EPR`), documents which are specific to a medical discipline (class `discipline specific document`), and documents that are related to a (small) process that is executed (class `process specific document`). Note that the generic document contains general medical data for a patient such as length, weight and blood pressure. In Fig. 4.12 some medical discipline specific documents for gastro-enterology (classes `gastroenterology document`, `gastro-enterology: colorectal carcinoma`, `gastro-enterology: examination of the body`, and `gastro-enterology: multidisciplinary meeting`) and cardiology (classes `cardiology`, `cardiology: MRT`, and `cardiology: TTE`) are shown. These documents are very specific and only a few examples are illustrated in Fig. 4.12.

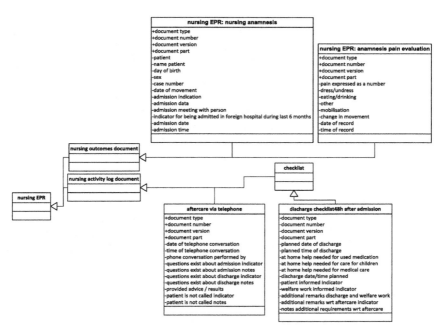

Fig. 4.11 Overview of the documents that are created by a nurse. These documents are either related to activities that are performed by a nurse (`nursing activity log document` class) or to outcomes of the nursing care that is provided (`nursing care outcomes document` class)

To illustrate process specific documents we list some documents that exist for the entire surgical process. This process starts from the moment that an order is created until the admission of the patient at the nursing ward. First, there are general surgery documents (class `surgery: general`) such as the `surgery: perioperative registration` document outlining general information regarding the entire surgical process. Second, there are documents for the preoperative phase. For example, the `surgery: anesthesia preoperative strategy` document contains information that is important before the surgery starts. Third, there are documents related to the surgery itself (class `surgery: surgery phase`). This may involve the materials and devices that are used (classes `surgery: technical devices` and `surgery: dressings /tamponades`), the anesthesia procedure (class `surgery: anesthesia procedure`), and the recording of events during the surgery (class `surgery: times registration`). Finally, there are the documents around the postoperative phase containing information that is important after surgery (e.g. the medication that is given (class `surgery: postoperative medication`)). Note that also for a physician checklists may exist (class `checklist`), e.g. a discharge checklist (class `discharge checklist`).

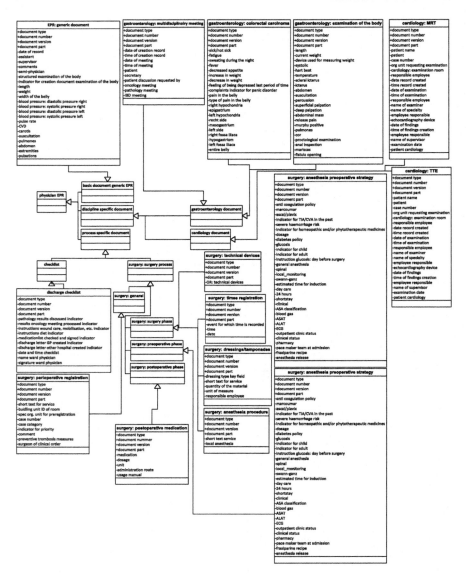

Fig. 4.12 Overview of the documents that are created by physicians. Here, generic documents exist (`basic document generic EPR` class), documents which are specific to a medical discipline (class `discipline specific document`), or documents that are related to a (small) process that is executed (`process specific document` class). Note that TTE is an abbreviation for Transthoracic Echocardiogram and MRT for Magnetic Resonance Tomography

Note that within the information system of MUMC there exist in total 550 different documents. From these documents there are 62 documents related to the surgery process. However, for each HIS the number of documents may be different. Above, we have indicated how these documents can be classified. Also, a few document types have been explicitly mentioned but there are many more.

4.2.7 Organization and Buildings

In Fig. 4.13, the classes corresponding to the organizational structure within the hospital and the structure of the buildings and rooms within the hospital can be found. First, the organizational unit class describes general information about an organizational unit such as its name, address, and whether it is an intensive care unit or outpatient clinic. In order to make some characteristics of an organizational unit clear it may be part of a category (class organizational unit category). Furthermore, this category can be used for indicating to which case types it may be assigned (class assignment org units to case types with associated multiplicity 0..*). Between multiple organizational units some relationships may exist (class relations between org units). Some examples of these relationships are the hierarchical structure that exists between organizational units (class hierarchy of organizational units) and the assignment of beds within an organizational unit by another organizational unit (class inter-dept. bed asgmts in an org unit by another org unit). The latter refers to the situation in which a certain organizational unit may use beds of another organizational unit in case all beds of that organizational unit are already occupied.

An organizational unit consists of multiple staff members. Some general characteristics of a staff member are described in the staff class (e.g. whether somebody is a nurse or a physician). As an organizational unit may consist of multiple staff members the multiplicity associated to the staff class is 1..*. A staff member should be part of at least one organizational unit which is denoted by the 1..* multiplicity attached to the organization unit class. For a staff member multiple attributes may exist (class attributes staff with associated multiplicity 0..*) such as its functions (class functions) and its roles (class roles). Note that for a staff member, the start and end of its job appointment is indicated. Also, the start of the validity of the rank is indicated.

In order for an organizational unit to perform its work, it may be allocated to multiple building units (class assignment building units to org units). Analogously to the organizational units, there are general characteristics for building units (class building units), additional attributes (class attributes building units with associated multiplicity 0..*), and relationships between building units (class relations between building units).

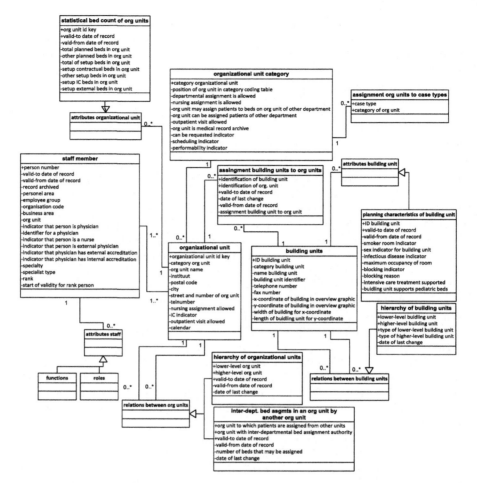

Fig. 4.13 The organizational structure within the hospital and the structure of the buildings and rooms within the hospital. For an organizational unit (organizational unit class), multiple kinds of attributes may exist (attributes organizational unit class) and relations with other organizational units can be defined (relations between org units class). Similarly, for a building unit (building units class) different kinds of attributes may be defined (attributes building units class) and relations with other building units (relation between building units class). Finally, an organizational unit may be linked with building units (assignment building units to org units class) and multiple staff members may be part of it (staff member class)

4.2.8 Nursing Plans

In Fig. 4.14 the corresponding classes for nursing plans are shown. In case a patient is admitted, nursing plans define the nursing care that is provided to a patient and his relatives. A nursing plan consists of the services that will be provided by a nurse in order to handle problems that are identified by a nursing assessment. A nursing plan (class `standard nursing plans`) may be part of a nursing plan profile (classes `assignment of standard nursing plan to nursing plan profile` and `nursing plan profiles`). Furthermore, for a nursing plan it is indicated which services are part of it (class `nursing standard plan - basic catalog assignment`).

With regard to a nursing plan, it is important that it can be individualized according to the specific needs of the patient. So, for each patient a selection is made from

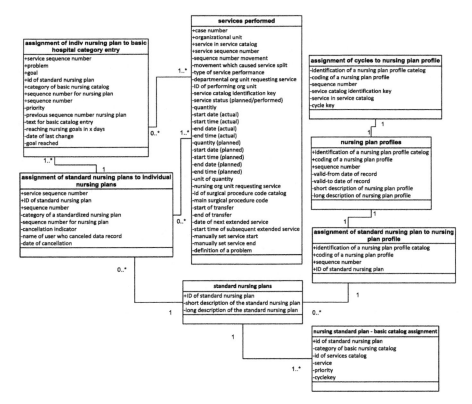

Fig. 4.14 Classes related to nursing plans. A nursing plan (`nursing plan class`) is part of a nursing plan profiles (`nursing plan profiles` class). A nursing plan is individualized to the needs of a patient and multiple services may be executed for it (`assignment of standard nursing plans to individual nursing plans` class)

the services that are part of a nursing plan. These selected services form together an individualized nursing plan (assignment of a standard nursing plan to individual nursing plans). Afterwards, the selected services are performed (class services performed).

4.2.9 Pathways

For many illnesses, guidelines exist in order to support in diagnosis and treating patients. The classes around the definition and assignment of these pathways can be found in Fig. 4.15.

General information concerning a pathway is described in the pathway class. Here, it is interesting that the period for which the pathway is valid is given. A pathway consists of multiple items of which the type may be different (class pathway item with associated multiplicity 1..*). More precisely, the types of the items depend on the language that has been chosen for modeling guidelines. For example, a type of item may refer to a specific service whereas another type may refer to a construct in order to split a process flow into multiple flows. An item may be connected with multiple other items but this is not required. This is indicated by the multiplicities 0..* of the associations that are attached to the connection class.

A pathway that is assigned to a patient is called a *patient pathway* (class patient pathway). Note that multiple patient pathways may be executed for a patient and that they are linked to either a patient (the associated multiplicity is 0..*) or a case (the associated multiplicity is 0..*). For a patient pathway, specific timing information is recorded such as its assignment, its (planned) start, and its (planned) completion. Also, state information about the start of the next step is recorded. Specific information about the execution of a step is described by the step of patient pathway class. In particular, for the execution of a step it is important that it is known whether it is executed, and by which step it is preceded and succeeded. Furthermore, timing information is recorded about the (planned) start, and execution of the step. Moreover, it is possible to connect a step with a performable service (classes connections with services performed and services performed). Finally, a step may be linked with medical documentation (class document created using pathways). Note that the execution of pathways is related to a series of steps for which it is desired that they are executed. For a patient many more steps may be executed of which their execution is saved as part of one of the classes in the "process steps" group.

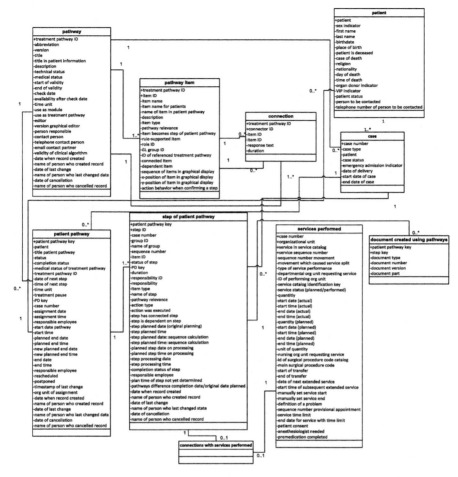

Fig. 4.15 The definition and execution of pathways. A pathway (`pathway` class) consists of multiple items (`pathway item` class) which may be connected to each other (`connection` class). A pathway is executed for a patient (`patient pathway` class) and information about each performed step is recorded (`step of patient pathway` class). Finally, each performed step may be linked to a service that is executed for the patient (`services performed` class)

4.3 Validation

In this section, we elaborate on the validation of the *healthcare reference model*. The main objective of the validation was to investigate whether the developed reference model is representative for data present in other hospitals. To this end, we investigated systems that were in use in hospitals other than the system that was used as basis for developing the reference model. Moreover, we discussed the reference model with several of their HIS professionals in order to identify missing data entities and to revise the model. Remember, that we validated our model in the AMC, Catharina, and Isala hospital.

As part of this undertaking, in total 22 classes were added to the reference model and 4 were removed. In order to give the reader an illustration of the considerations taken into account during validation we focus on the medication (Sect. 4.2.3) and document data (Sect. 4.2.6) classes. For these two groups of classes some major changes were made.

In the original model for "Medication" there were 7 classes whereas in the updated reference model there are 12 classes. In particular, the drug, drug formulary, and drug event - drug assignment classes were added in order to distinguish that a drug order may consist of multiple drugs that are prescribed. Furthermore, the dosage quantities infusions class was added as a drug order may consist of multiple infusions that are given. Finally, the preparation of administration documentation of event class was added as for some drugs it may be needed to do some preparations before they are administered. The above mentioned class changes were identified when discussing the reference model with specialists of the AMC hospital that were responsible for the medication system. For the added classes it was also checked whether the same information was present in the system of the MUMC that was investigated in order to develop the reference model. As this was the case, the classes were added to the model.

In the original model for "Document Data" there were 33 classes whereas in the updated reference model there are 47 classes. In particular, we made three major changes. First, we added a class with regard to the medical documents. In the old version of the reference model, we made a distinction between documentation that is created by a physician (class physician EPR) and documentation that is created by a nurse (class nursing EPR). In the updated model it is also distinguished that documentation can be provided by a allied health professional (class allied health profession EPR). This change was triggered during a discussion with health professionals of Isala. As such a distinction could also be made for MUMC, AMC, and Catharina, the classes were added to the model.

Second, for a nurse, in the revised model, a distinction is made into documents that relate to activities that are performed by a nurse (nursing activity log document class) and documents that relate to outcomes of the nursing care that is provided (nursing outcomes document class). This distinction emerged after inspection of the GUI of AMC's EPR system. After discussion with professionals of the three other hospitals it was decided to update the model.

Finally, for both a nurse and a physician a further specialization in the form of checklists is created. When discussing this concept with the professionals of the four hospitals it was identified that the usage of checklists in hospitals is growing. Moreover, all four hospitals already provided support for checklists in their systems. As a consequence, four classes were added (classes checklist and discharge checklist 48h after admission in Fig. 4.11 and classes checklist and discharge checklist in Fig. 4.12) to the reference model.

In general, discussions with HIS professionals led to important insights for improving the *healthcare reference model*. Furthermore, interacting with the GUI of some systems also triggered discussions about the validity of the reference model. In principle, HISs that are provided by software suppliers, other than the ones investigated by us, may contain data and functionalities that are not present within our reference model. However, we feel that by following the above mentioned approach, the developed *healthcare reference model* may considered to be representative for key data of other HIS implementations.

References

1. Object Management Group. *OMG Unified Modeling Language, Version 2.0.* Object Management Group, 2005
2. E.N. de Vies, H.A. Prins, R.M.P.H. Crolla, A.J. den Outer, G. van Andel, S.H. van Helden, W.S. Schlack, M.A. van Putten, D.J. Gouma, M.G.W. Dijkgraaf, S.M. Smorenburg, and M.A. Boermeester. Effect of a Comprehensive Surgical Safety System on Patient Outcomes. *The New England Journal Medicine*, 363:1928–1937, 2010

Chapter 5
Applications of Process Mining

Abstract The healthcare reference model illustrates the wealth of event data available in today's hospitals. In this chapter, we focus on the application of process mining using such data. We identify various process mining use cases. These illustrate the use of process mining techniques like process discovery and conformance checking based on the healthcare reference model. We use event data from the Maastricht University Medical Center (MUMC) and the Academic Medical Center (AMC) in Amsterdam to illustrate the process mining use cases. The examples demonstrate that tools like ProM can indeed be used to remove inefficiencies and improve quality.

Keywords Process mining use cases · Process discovery · Conformance checking · Process mining · Healthcare · Healthcare reference model

From the previous section, it can be concluded that a HIS holds an enormous amount of data. Based on the *healthcare reference model* it is possible to generate many logs each focusing on different (parts of) processes. For these logs, the recorded process steps may reside at different levels of granularity. Some examples of possible processes that may be investigated are:

- The process that is performed by gastro-enterology and surgery in order to treat rectal cancer patients. In particular, the focus is on medical services that are performed such as a CT-scan, a surgery for removing a part of the intestines, and a visit to the outpatient clinic.
- The process for supporting the patient and his relatives. This involves non-medical services such informing the relatives of the patient or the handing out of brochures.
- The surgical care process. This involves the process which starts at the moment the clinical order for the surgery is created until the patient is admitted at the ward after surgery. Note that this involves process steps which reside at different levels of aggregation. It encompasses the pre-operative assessment but also the entire lower-level process starting from the moment that the patient is transported to the surgical department until the arrival in the recovery room.
- The process of a patient visiting the outpatient clinic. This may involve events such as "arrival patient", "start visit to physician", "end visit to physician", and "departure patient".

- The process related to the services that are delivered by nurses at a specific patient ward.
- The process for transporting patients within the hospital.

In this section, the possibilities of process mining within a typical hospital are illustrated. We first assume that the data described in the reference model are indeed available and that no data quality issues apply, i.e., data are assumed to be complete and correct. Given this, we give examples of process mining analyses that are possible. In particular, we want to focus on analyses that are particularly interesting for the healthcare domain. We show that analyses can be performed for the different kinds of processes visualized in Fig. 2.1 in Chap. 2. Two large data sets that were obtained based on the *healthcare reference model* are used for this purpose. To be more precise, from two large university hospitals in the Netherlands, MUMC and AMC, data were obtained.

First, more details will be provided regarding the data sets of MUMC and AMC. Then, we focus on the different kinds of analyses that are possible. The different types of analysis are presented in the form of use cases.

5.1 Data Set from the Maastricht University Medical Center

In this section, we provide more details about the data that were obtained from the Maastricht University Medical Center (MUMC). The data contained information about two different patient groups that have been treated in the hospital. One patient group concerns 296 gastro-enterology patients suffering from intestinal cancer and one patient group concerns 1206 ophthalmology patients suffering from cataract. Both patient groups were treated in the period of 2008 until 2013. In total, data were extracted from 60 different tables. In this section, we indicate for which classes from the *healthcare reference model* data were obtained. Moreover, we provide a snippet of the real data for some classes in order to illustrate the raw data that are present in the *healthcare reference model*.

Figure 5.1 illustrates the data obtained for the "general patient and case data" and "process steps" groups of the *healthcare reference model*. More precisely, for each group the name of each class is given in a separate rectangle and the relationships between these rectangles are similar as for the classes in the respective group. In Fig. 5.1 it is also indicated for each class how many rows are present in the corresponding table in the data set. If no data were obtained for a particular class this is indicated by a grey colored rectangle and the "no records" text in it. By definition, for all classes which are a generalization of other classes no data were obtained: concrete data are associated to the more specific classes. Note that these classes are visualized by a white rectangle in which the name is written in italics. For example, Fig. 5.1a shows that for the `case` and `complications` classes of the "general patient and case data" group, 10,751 and 468 records were obtained respectively. For the `health problems` and `logging for VIP patients` classes, no data were obtained. Figure 5.1b shows that for the `movements` and `services performed` classes

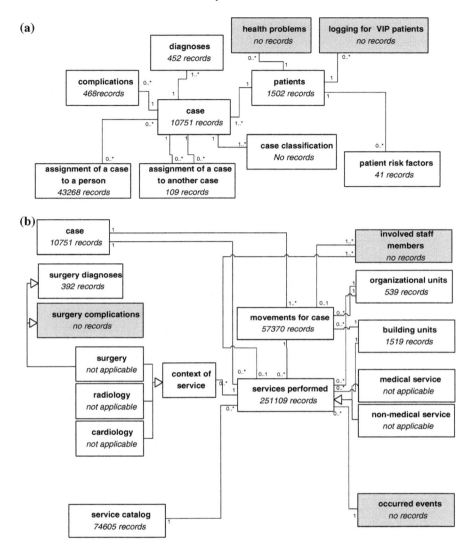

Fig. 5.1 For both the "general patient and case data" and the "process steps" groups of the *healthcare reference model* it is shown for which classes data have been obtained from the *i.s.h.med* system of the MUMC. **a** Data obtained for the 'general patient and case data' group (see Fig. 4.2). **b** Data obtained for the 'different kind of process steps' subgroup of the 'processes and process steps' group (see Fig. 4.4)

of the "different kinds of process steps" subgroup of the "process steps" group, 57,370 and 251,109 records were obtained respectively. For the context of service class no data were obtained as it is a generalization of the surgery, radiology, and cardiology classes. Furthermore, also data for the "document data", "nursing plans", and "organization and buildings" groups of the *healthcare reference model* were obtained.

Figure 5.2 provides more detailed insights into the data that are present in the *healthcare reference model*. More precisely, for the "general patient and case data" group and the "process steps" group, two snippets are provided of the data that were obtained. Note that the data are anonymized in order to maintain confidentiality. Regarding the data for the `patient` class of the "general patient and case data" group, we show for example that patient "p1" is Dutch and has deceased. Moreover, the religion field shows value "02" which means that the patient was Roman Catholic. For the `services performed` class of the "process steps" group it can be seen that service "v1" was started and completed at "30-10-2011".

(a)

patient identifier	date when record created	date when record created	country of birth	cause of death	patient is deceased	marital status	ethnical group	religion	sex indicator	nationality	langu age	coun try
Patiënt	Invoer datum	Datum laatste wijz	Gebland patiënt	Doods oorzaak	Tk pat overlede	Burgerlijke staat	Etnische groep	Religie	Geslacht	Nationaliteit	Taal	Land
p1	06/02/2009	21/07/2012			X			02	1			NL
p2	06/02/2009	07/10/2010							1			NL
p3	06/02/2009	13/04/2012						02	1			NL
p4	06/02/2009	03/10/2012						12	1			NL
p5	13/11/2009	03/12/2009							2	NL		NL
p6	12/10/2010	10/11/2010	NL						1	NL		NL
p7	06/02/2009	03/05/2012						02	1		NL	NL
p8	06/02/2009	22/06/2012			X			12	2			NL
p9	06/02/2009	31/12/2012			X			02	1			NL

(b)

service sequence number	time service performance ends	partial delivery quantity of service	date when record created	created by employee	case	time service performance starts	date of last change	cancellation indicator	ZAT-code	performing medical discipline
Volgnr verrichting	Einddatum Verr	Deel hoeveelheid	Gecreëerd op	Gecreëerd door	Ziekte geval	Begindatum Verr	Gewijzigd op	Storno teken	ZAT-code	Int Uitvoerend Spec
v1	30/10/2011	0	07/11/2011	t1	c1	30/10/2011	09/06/2012		0000074896	KCH
v2	30/10/2011	0	07/11/2011	t1	c1	30/10/2011	09/06/2012		0000070419	KCH
v3	30/10/2011	0	07/11/2011	t1	c1	30/10/2011	09/06/2012		0000070116	KCH
v4	30/10/2011	0	07/11/2011	t1	c1	30/10/2011	09/06/2012		0000070402	KCH
v5	30/10/2011	0	07/11/2011	t1	c1	30/10/2011	09/06/2012		0000074110	KCH

requesting medical discipline	treating medical discipline	Indicator for dummy service	service payable	date of cancellation	record modified by employee	movement	performing org unit	requesting nursing org unit	requesting org unit
Int Aanvragend Spec	Int Behandelend Spec	Teken: Dummy Verrich	Kosten drverricht	Gestorneerd door	Gewijzigd door	Beweging	Uitvoerende OE	Aanvr verpl OE	Aanvr spec OE
INT	KCH		X		f1	6	LCHE	PEHU	SAIG
INT	KCH		X		f1	6	LCHE	PEHU	SAIG
INT	KCH		X		f1	6	LCHE	PEHU	SAIG
INT	KCH		X		f1	6	LCHE	PEHU	SAIG
INT	KCH		X		f1	6	LCHE	PEHU	SAIG

service	service in service catalog	patient	performing physician	anesthesiologist
Verrichting	Verricht catalogus	Patiënt	Uitvoerend Arts	Anesthesist
0000370423	RG	p1	a1	
0000370419	RG	p1	a1	
0000370403	RG	p1	a1	
0000370402	RG	p1	a1	
0000370401	RG	p1	a1	

Fig. 5.2 Some snippets of the data that have been obtained from the *i.s.h.med* system in use at the MUMC. For each column the Dutch description has been provided. **a** Snippet of the data that has been obtained for the *patient* class of the 'general patient and case data' group (Fig. 4.2). **b** Snippet of the data that has been obtained for the *services performed* class of the 'process steps' group (Fig. 4.4)

Moreover, as requesting medical discipline the value "INT" was filled in which refers to the "internal medicine" discipline. Note that for several columns in both snippets only identifiers are given (e.g. "religion", "sex indicator", "performing medical discipline", "requesting medical discipline", and "performing org unit"). For each of these columns a corresponding table exists in the *i.s.h.med* system in which more details are provided for the identifiers that are used in the column (e.g. a description).

5.2 Data Set from the Academic Medical Center

In this section, we give more details about the data that were obtained from the Academic Medical Center (AMC). This data set contains information about 232 ophthalmology patients suffering from cataract. The patients were treated in the period of 2010 till 2013. In total, data were extracted from 14 different tables. In a similar fashion as for the MUMC data set we indicate for which classes from the reference model data were obtained. Also, a snippet of the real data is shown for some of the classes.

Figure 5.3a indicates the data that were obtained for the "Orders and Appointments" subgroup of the "process steps" group. For example, for the `patients` and `appointments` classes, 232 and 3249 records were obtained respectively. In Fig. 5.3b, a snippet of the data of the `appointments` class is shown. Again data were anonymized in order to maintain confidentiality. For example, patient "p1" has an appointment at 02/05/2011 from 10:15 till 10:40 performed by resource "r1". The appointment is a regular visit ("consultation type") and scheduled on 07/04/2011 by resource "r10". For some of the columns (e.g. "afspraak" and "consult") a corresponding table exists in the system in which more details are provided for the identifiers that are used in the column.

5.3 Process Mining Use Cases

In this section, we elaborate on the application opportunities of process mining that make use of data of the *healthcare reference model*. In particular, we focus on the types of analyses that are most interesting for the healthcare domain and illustrate possible types of process mining analyses. Additionally, these use cases help in demonstrating the applicability of the reference model.

Figure 5.4 shows a graphical presentation of the six use cases that are described below. All use cases have been performed using ProM 6.[1] A log is depicted using a rectangle containing lines, a model is depicted using a pentagon, and a feature set is depicted using only a rectangle.

---

[1] www.processmining.org.

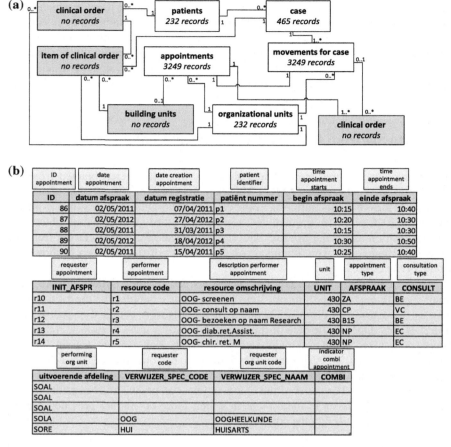

Fig. 5.3 For the "Orders and Appointments" subgroup of the "process steps" group of the *healthcare reference model* it is shown for which classes data have been obtained from the system of the AMC. Additionally, for the `appointments` class a snippet of the data are shown. **a** Data obtained for the 'orders and appointments' subgroup of the 'process steps group' (Fig. 4.5). **b** Snippet of the data that has been obtained for the *appointment* class of the 'orders and appointments' group (Fig. 4.5)

5.3.1 Use Case 1: Exploring Selections of Events

The focus of this use case is on exploring a selection of events. During this analysis, it is important to decide on a specific scope, i.e., the classes of the *healthcare reference model* events need to selected from and the events that are most important in these classes. Process mining analyses are executed which allow for getting a visual view on the characteristics of the data (e.g. the dotted chart [1], the Basic Performance Analysis plug-in) and for obtaining initial process related insights (e.g. the heuristics miner [2] and the fuzzy miner [3]).

Fig. 5.4 Use cases of
applying process mining in
the healthcare domain. The
use cases are based on the
healthcare reference model

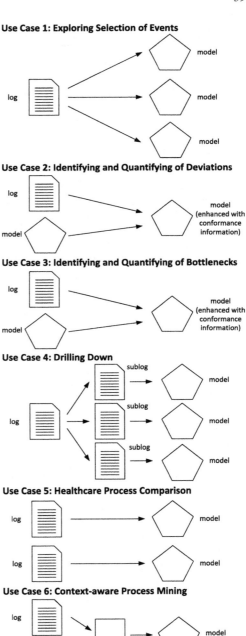

In order to illustrate this use case, we take data of MUMC regarding 296 gastro-enterology patients suffering from intestinal cancer. In terms of Fig. 2.1 (Chap. 2), the process for these patients can be considered elective and non-routine. The physician proceeds in a step-by-step way: checking the patient's reaction to an individual treatment and deciding on the steps to be taken next. Although it is important that treatment is started as quickly as possible it is not required that care is provided immediately.

Figures 5.5 and 5.6 illustrate this use case. Figure 5.5a shows that data have been obtained from the `services performed`, `organizational units`, `building units`, and `medical service` classes. For the group of gastro-enterology patients, we selected the services that were performed for the patients suffering from large intestine cancer until the surgical intervention. In total, this resulted in a log with 105 patients, 6225 events, and 516 event classes.

Both Fig. 5.5b, c show a dotted chart which visualizes events as dots. As such, a "helicopter view" of the process is obtained and patterns can be discovered. On the vertical axis the different cases (i.e., patients) are shown and events are colored according to their activity names. In Fig. 5.5b, the process is shown using actual time, i.e., all cases are sorted based on the first event that took place. As can be seen from the chart, the arrival pattern of patients is pretty stable. However, there are periods in which only a few patients arrive (e.g. June/July 2010) or periods in which more patients arrive (e.g. March 2010 till June 2010). In Fig. 5.5c, the process is shown using relative time, i.e., all cases start at time zero. The chart shows that for a small group of patients the time until surgery is much longer. For 26 out of the 105 patients the time until surgery is more than 60 days. This group of patients turned out to be complex cases for which an individualized treatment was necessary. For the majority of patients the time until surgery is less than 60 days. Also, the variation is small as shown by the steep line in the chart.

For getting the first process related insights, it was decided to include only the patients for which the time until surgery was less then 60 days. Also, we focused on the most frequent events. In this way, we did not obtain an overly complex model when applying a control-flow discovery algorithm. In Figs. 5.6a and 5.7a, b, the discovered models by respectively the fuzzy miner, the heuristics miner, and the inductive miner are shown. In all models, the services performed and the ordering of these services can be seen. The miners have been chosen as they can deal with noise and exceptions, and enables users to focus on the main process flow instead of on every detail of the behavior appearing in the process log.

The three models reveal some clear causal relations between services. Note that for the fuzzy miner the significance of a relation between two services are indicated by the thickness of the corresponding edge between these services, i.e., more significant relations have a wider edge. As important causal relations we find in all models that the "preoperative assessment" service is followed by the "admission hospital" service. After, the admission there is either a "hemicolectomy", "transversectomy", or "subtotal colectomy" surgery. Moreover, the fuzzy miner shows that after the "coloscopy" there is a "histological examination". On the other hand, the inductive miner shows that these activities occur in parallel. In addition, the fuzzy miner shows

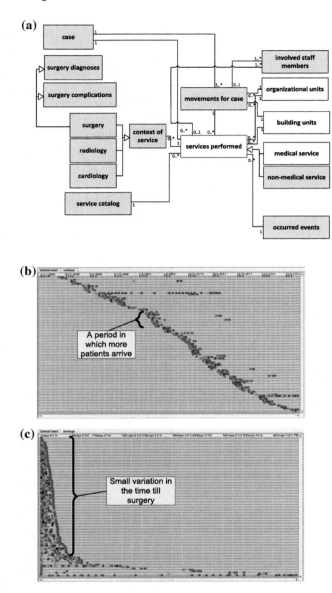

Fig. 5.5 The data and some results that have been obtained during the "exploring selections of events" analysis. **a** Overview of the classes of the 'different kind of process steps' subgroup of the 'process steps' group (Fig. 4.4) for which data has been taken in order to perform the 'exploring selections of events' and 'constructing a precise model' analysis. **b** Dotted chart for the process till surgery. All cases start at their real time. **c** Dotted chart for the process till surgery. All cases start at time zero

(a)   **(b)**

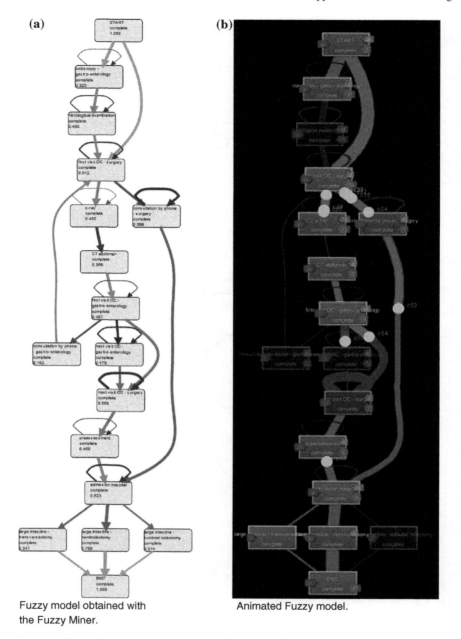

Fuzzy model obtained with   Animated Fuzzy model.
the Fuzzy Miner.

Fig. 5.6 Two models showing the discovered control-flow for the group of 89 patients suffering from large intestine cancer. **a** Fuzzy model obtained with the fuzzy miner. **b** Animated fuzzy model

(a)

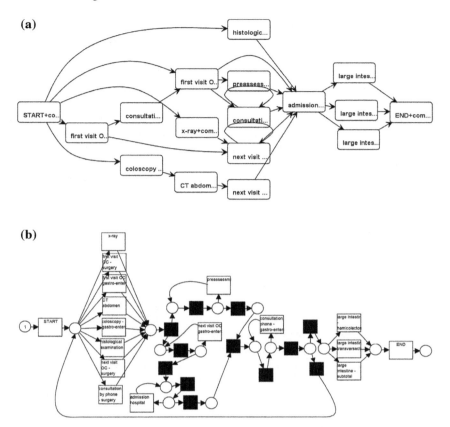

(b)

Fig. 5.7 Two models showing the discovered control-flow for the group of 89 patients suffering from large intestine cancer. **a** Heuristics net obtained with the heuristics miner. **b** Petri net obtained with the inductive miner

that after the "histological examination" there is a first visit to the outpatient clinic of surgery ("first visit OC—surgery" service). Also, after the first visit to the outpatient clinic of surgery an "X-ray" occurs and after the "X-ray" a "CT-abdomen" occurs.

In addition to showing a process model, the fuzzy miner has two other interesting features. First, the brightness of edges between nodes emphasizes their correlation, i.e., more correlated relations are darker. For example, for the "X-ray" and "CT abdomen" services it is indicated in the model that they are highly correlated. In this case, dependent on the chosen settings for the fuzzy miner, it is indicated that the temporal proximity between these services is high.

Second, the fuzzy miner offers a dynamic view of the process by replaying the log in the model. The animation shows cases flowing through the model (depicted as dots in Fig. 5.6b). In the animation, frequently taken paths are highlighted, which prevents them from being overlooked. As a result, users can easily see how various parts of the model perform in real life, simply by observing the animation. This makes it straightforward to pinpoint performance bottlenecks in the process, or to identify those parts in the process that are most heavily executed. For example, the animated part of the log visualized in Fig. 5.6b) shows that the path leading from the "first visit OC—surgery" event to the "X-ray" event is frequently taken. Moreover, the animation shows how things can change over time.

As a result of the analysis, it turned out that several patients (with long overall throughput times) fall outside the scope and that some clear causal relationships exist between several activities. Using the above mentioned analyses these things can obviously be identified.

The models produced by a process mining algorithm provide clear insights and show the way the process was actually executed. However, depending on the goal of the analysis it may be needed to (semi-)automatically tailor a discovered model to better satisfy certain requirements. Examples of these requirements are that the obtained model is a good reflection of the behavior captured in the log (i.e., the model fits the log), the obtained model is simple, or the model allows only minimally more behavior than seen in the log.

For illustrating the construction of a precise model, we focus on the approach that has been used for coming to a precise model based on the control-flow models that were obtained as part of the previous analysis (Fig. 5.6). Here, it is important that medical professionals are often interested in learning about the performance of the process in order to identify the bottlenecks in the process. In order to reliably enrich a given (discovered) model with performance information it is important that the precise model is a good reflection of the behavior captured in the log. So, first the model obtained by the heuristics miner was converted into a Petri net. Based on the additional insights shown in the fuzzy model, the Petri net model was adapted by hand and it was checked in the process mining tool ProM how well it reflected the behavior in the log. This second step was repeated until the model was a good reflection of the behavior captured in the log. The resulting Petri net model is shown in Fig. 5.8. Note that the Petri net is annotated with diagnostics generated by the conformance checker plug-in.

The main characteristics of the process of Fig. 5.8 can be described as follows. First, a coloscopy ("coloscopy") takes place followed by a histological examination ("histological examination"), if needed, or the patient immediately visits the outpatient clinic of surgery ("first visit OC—surgery"). After, the visit to the outpatient clinic of surgery, both a CT abdomen ("CT abdomen") and X-ray ("X-ray") is performed followed by a next consultation at the outpatient clinic ("next visit OC—gastro-enterology" and "next visit OC—surgery") or a consultation by phone ("consultation by phone—gastro-enterology"). Subsequently, a preassessment ("preassessment") takes place and a next consultation, if needed, before the patient is admitted to the hospital ("admission surgery" service). Next, a surgery on the large intestine takes place ("large intestine—hemicolectomy", "large intestine—subtotal colectomy", and "large intestine—transversectomy"). As shown in the model, there are some parts in the process where the process does not conform with the log. For

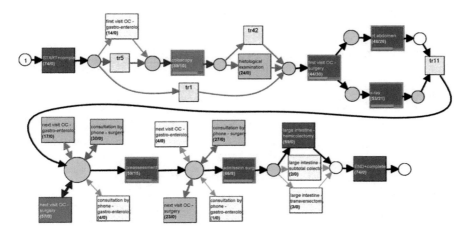

Fig. 5.8 The Petri net model that has been obtained during the analysis. Using the "conformance analysis" plug-in of ProM it was checked whether the adapted model reflected the behavior in the model well

example, not always both a CT abdomen and a X-ray are made after the first visit to the outpatient clinic of surgery.

Altogether, this analysis illustrates how to come to a model which is a good reflection of the behavior captured in the log. We deliberately abstracted from the technical details of the discovery techniques and refer to [2] for more information.

5.3.2 Use Case 2: Identifying and Quantifying Deviations

For this use case, the aim is to investigate the conformance between a given process model and an event log. As such, tasks in the model are identified that should have occurred but did not occur in reality ("move on model") or tasks are identified that have occurred in reality although these tasks were not anticipated in the model ("move on log"). Besides identifying the aforementioned deviations, they are also quantified.

In order to illustrate this use case, data were obtained from the `occurred events` class as shown in Fig. 5.9. More precisely, for the group of 79 patients of the previous use case, we obtained all the events that are registered in the context of a surgery that is performed. This involves events between the transportation of the patient to the surgery department until the arrival in the recovery room. In total, the log contained 79 patients, 767 events, and 17 event classes. Note that the recording of events is done manually. Furthermore, for the events that need to be registered in the aforementioned period, a "normative" process model exists which describes the events that need to be recorded and the ordering of them.

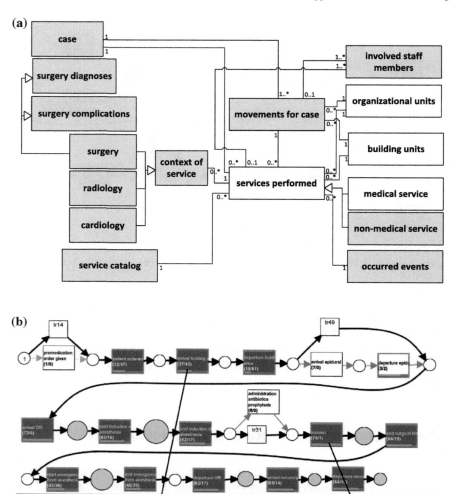

Fig. 5.9 For a group of 79 patients conformance information is collected for the events that need to registered in the context of a surgery that takes place. **a** Overview of the classes of the 'process steps' group (Fig. 4.4) for which data has been taken in order to perform the 'identifying and qualifying deviations' analysis. **b** Obtained Petri net annotated with diagnostics generated by the conformance checker plugin

In Fig. 5.9, the model is shown together with diagnostic information about the deviations between the log and the model. As shown in the figure, the process starts with a premedication order if needed ("premedication order given"). Subsequently, the patient is ordered and the patient arrives in the holding area in order to be prepared for surgery ("arrival holding area" and "departure holding area"). Next, the patient may need to be transported to a different room in order to allow for epidural anesthesia ("arrival epidural" and "departure epidural"). Shortly before surgery, the patient is transported to the surgery room ("arrival OR") after which the anesthesia team starts the induction of the anesthesia ("start induction of anesthesia"). Subsequently, there is the option to provide an antibiotic prophylaxis treatment ("administration antibiotica prophylaxis"). The surgery starts with the incision ("incision") and finishes with the closure of the tissue with stitches ("end surgical time"). Next, the anesthesia team performs the emergence from the anesthesia ("start emergency from anesthesia"), which ends when the patient has regained consciousness ("end emergency from anesthesia"). Subsequently, the patient leaves the operating room ("departure OR") and is transported to the recovery room ("arrival recovery"). Once the patient is stable enough, the patient is transported from the recovery room to the nursing ward ("departure recovery").

As the events in the model are recorded manually, there are several deviations between the model and the log. In order to identify and quantify these deviations the model is annotated with diagnostic information by the conformance checker plug-in. More precisely, for each transition the ratio is given between the cases for which there existed a corresponding event during replay of the transition (the green colored bar) and the cases for which there was no matching event during replay of the transition (the purple colored bar). The size of the yellow colored places indicates for the respective state in the model the number of cases in which for the event to be replayed no matching transition could be found. For example, it can be seen that the "incision" event most often has been registered correctly whereas for the "departure holding area" this was exactly the opposite.

Next to that, the conformance checker allows for checking for each patient which parts of the model could be successfully replayed and which not. For example, for 5 cases it was found that the "patient ordered", "arrival holding area", and "departure holding area" events were not recorded although this is mandatory. Also, via the plug-in it was discovered that the average fitness was only 0.77 (note that the minimal value is "0" and the maximal value is "1") and that there were no cases which could be successfully replayed. Overall, during the analysis it becomes clear that due to the manual registration many events are not registered or registered in the wrong order. Based on the conformance analysis, deviations that need further investigation are identified.

5.3.3 Use Case 3: Identifying and Quantifying Bottlenecks

In healthcare, a lot of attention is paid to preventing unnecessary waiting times. As such it is important that time-related performance information can be obtained for a healthcare process. The focus of this use case is on the identification and quantification of time-related bottlenecks within the process.

Figure 5.10 illustrates this use case. The constructed event log contains data from the `items of clinical order`, `appointments`, and `organizational units` classes. For the group of 79 patients of the "exploring selections of events" analysis type, we now collected information about the steps that are performed in the context of ordering and organizing all appointments that are needed for a surgical intervention and producing the surgical report. This process is depicted in Fig. 5.10b. First, an order is created for the surgery ("order"). On the basis of this order, a pre-assessment is scheduled ("preassessment schedule") and performed ("preassessment complete"). The surgery order is also followed by the appointment for surgery ("surgery schedule"), the admission to the hospital ("admission hospital"), and the surgical procedure itself. With regard to the surgical procedure a distinction has been made between the scheduled start of the surgery ("surgery scheduled start"), the actual start of the surgery ("surgery start"), and the actual completion of the surgery ("surgery complete"). Finally, after the surgical procedure, a surgical report is created ("surgery report start") and finalized afterwards ("surgery report complete"). Note that obtaining execution data for this process involved collecting data from several classes of the *healthcare reference model*. More specifically, execution data regarding the "order" task were collected from the *item of clinical order* class, execution data for the "preassessment start", "preassessment complete", "surgery schedule", and "surgery scheduled start" tasks were collected from the *appointments* class, and execution data regarding the "surgery start", "surgery complete", "surgery report start", and "surgery report complete" tasks were obtained from the *reports surgery* class. In total, this resulted in a log with 79 patients, 639 events, and 11 event classes. Clearly, the *healthcare reference model* was of great help for identifying the existence of the aforementioned kinds of information and for the subsequent creation of the event log.

For the process of Fig. 5.10c, performance information is projected by coloring the places and the transitions. A red colored transition or place indicates a high average waiting time whereas on the other end of the spectrum a white colored transition or place indicates a low average waiting time. When inspecting the figure, several important insights can be obtained. For example, after scheduling a surgery, it still takes on average 17.80 days (standard deviation: 7.66 days) before the patient is admitted to the hospital. Also, on average there are 5.63 days (standard deviation: 7.07 days) between the creation of the order and the scheduling of an appointment for the surgery. Finally, 17.96 h (standard deviation: 1.46 days) are spend on average between the completion of the surgery and the creation of the surgery report.

As a result of the analysis, some obvious performance bottlenecks are identified. This kind of information is crucial for determining effective measures for improving the efficiency of the process.

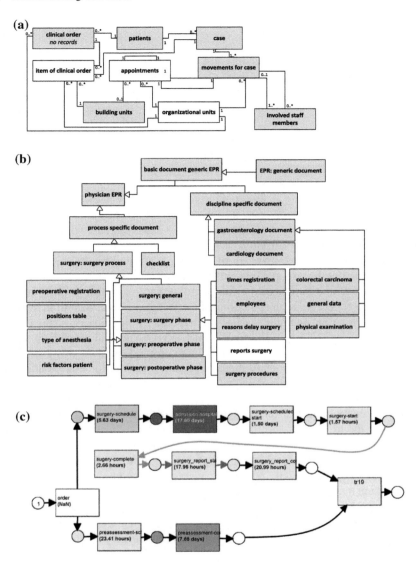

Fig. 5.10 For a group of 79 patients performance information is collected for the process of ordering and organizing the steps that need to be done for a surgical intervention. **a** Overview of the classes of the 'orders and appointments' subgroup of the 'process steps' group (Fig. 4.5) for which data has been taken in order to perform the 'identifying and qualifying bottlenecks' analysis. **b** Overview of the classes of the 'document data' group for which data has been taken in order to perform the 'identifying and qualifying bottlenecks' analysis. **c** Obtained Petri net annotated with performance information generated by the conformance checker plugin. A *red colored* transition indicates a high average waiting time for the respective event whereas on the other end of the spectrum a *light yellow colored* transition indicates a low average waiting time for the respective event

5.3.4 Use Case 4: Drilling Down

Given the outcome of a certain analysis it may be desired to further drill down into the data in order to investigate a (part of a) process in more detail. This drilling down can be done according to different dimensions. One dimension is the *case type* dimension in which cases are selected that satisfy a certain property (e.g. the cases that are late). Another dimension is the *event class* dimension which involves the selection of events satisfying certain properties (e.g. the name or resource of the event). Also, the *time* dimension can be used for focusing on a certain time window (e.g. a particular week or the activities performed in the first half year).

Examples of process mining techniques for further drilling down into the data are clustering techniques (e.g. the guide tree miner [4]) or decision point analysis techniques (e.g. the decision point analysis plug-in [5]). Moreover, within ProM several log filtering techniques can be used to drill down (e.g. the LTL checker [6]).

Figure 5.11 shows an illustration of this use case. Here, we further drill down into the analysis that is performed for the group of 79 patients suffering from large intestine cancer. For this group of patients the associated process is shown in Fig. 5.8. In Fig. 5.11a the distribution of the time until surgery is shown for this group of patients. In the Netherlands, the guideline of the Dutch cancer association, regarding an acceptable time between the start of the trajectory until surgery, states that this should be at most 35 days. In the figure, these 35 days are indicated by a vertical black line. As becomes clear, for a quite a large group of patients this guideline is violated (34 patients). In order to identify possible reasons for this violation, the process followed by this group of patients is investigated in further detail. Therefore, in Fig. 5.11b performance information has been projected in line with the "identifying and quantifying bottlenecks" analysis type. In Fig. 5.11c the associated frequency is depicted for the transitions and the places. A red color indicates a high frequency whereas on the other end of the spectrum a white color indicates a low frequency. Both models make clear that there is a high waiting time for the admission to the hospital ("admission hospital" transition, average: 12.88 days, standard deviation: 7.55 days) and that this transition is also often executed (31 times). Also, for the next visit to the outpatient clinic of surgery ("next visit OC—surgery" transition, average: 5.73 days, standard deviation: 2.50 days, occurrence: 39) and a consultation by phone of the surgery department ("consultation by phone—surgery" transition, average: 5.85 days, standard deviation: 4.44 days, occurrence: 28) there are reasonable high waiting times and the occurrence of these activities is also high. So, in order to improve the average throughput time of the entire process it needs to be investigated whether the average waiting time of these three activities can be reduced. Altogether, the drilling-down functionality supports a focused and detailed analysis approach.

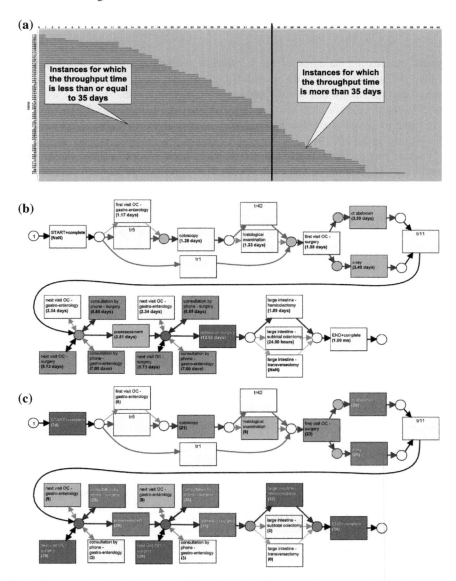

Fig. 5.11 At the *top* for the group of 79 patients (see Fig. 5.8) the distribution of the time until surgery is given. Subsequently, for these patients for which the time till surgery is more than 35 days, in the *middle*, the process model is annotated with information about the average waiting time for both transitions and places. At the *bottom*, the process model is annotated with information about the frequency of both transitions and places. **a** Distribution of the throughput time of the instances. At the *right* of the *black line* the throughput time is more than 35 days. **b** For each transition and place the average waiting time is visualized. **c** For each transition and place the frequency is visualized

5.3.5 Use Case 5: Healthcare Process Comparison

Another interesting outcome of the *healthcare reference model* is that processes of different hospitals can be compared. So, given a selected patient group it can be ensured that the same data are collected in various hospitals. As a next step, a process model is discovered for each hospital and then they are compared with each other.

In order to demonstrate this use case, data were collected for cataract patients for both MUMC and AMC. In terms of Fig. 2.1 (Chap. 2), a cataract process is an elective and routine care process. Treatment may be postponed for one or more weeks and it is well-known which steps need to be performed during diagnosis and treatment.

Figure 5.12 shows that data were obtained from the movements for case, services performed, and organizational units classes. For the MUMC, a log was constructed with data on 1434 patients, 40,802 events, and 348 event classes. For the AMC, the log contains 232 patients, 4796 events, and 56 event classes. For both logs preprocessing was applied to ensure that only events regarding diagnosis and treatment steps are present. For example, events referring to the nursing care provided during an admission are removed. As a next step, we selected for both logs the top 5 % of most occurring events in order to not end up with cluttered process models.

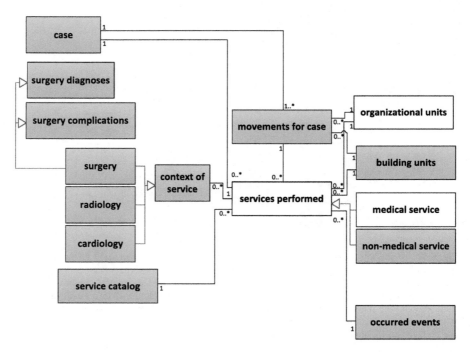

Fig. 5.12 Overview of the classes of the *healthcare reference model* for which data have been obtained for both the MUMC and AMC hospital

One of the challenges during the analysis was that in the two different hospitals different names were used for the same movement or service. Here, we could make use of the fact that in the Netherlands a coding scheme is used for identifying similar activities. So, although activity names may differ between hospitals they can be recognized to be the same as they have a similar code. For example, for activity "next visit OC" as code "190013" is used. Using this code, for MUMC the "Vervolgconsult algemeen" activity and for AMC the "VERVOLGCONSULT POLIKLINISCH" activity could me matched.

For comparison, process models capturing patient flows need to faithfully reflect the behaviors captured in the log, i.e., the fitness of the models need to be high. To this end, we used a similar approach as in the second use case. The discovered models are shown in Fig. 5.13. At the top, the model for the MUMC is shown and the AMC model is shown at the bottom. The red rectangles in the figure highlight the main differences with regard to the activities performed and the ordering of the activities. In general, both the model of MUMC and AMC can be divided into three parts. The first part, visualized by observation "O1" represents the first visit of the patient ("first visit OC") and a series of diagnostic tests that are performed. The second part, visualized by observation "O2", represents the patient's admission for surgery and the surgical procedure itself. After discharge, the patient again has several tests before a next surgery (to the other eye) or ends up in the aftercare trajectory in which the hospital is regularly visited and several tests are performed. This latter part is visualized by observation "O3".

Next, the thee main observations are described in detail.

Observation 1 (O1):   For the series of diagnostic tests after the first visit it can be seen that five activity names are shared. The "corneal topography" and "emergency care" activities are only performed by MUMC. Within AMC only the "vision range examination", "YAG laser coagulation", "lab test", "hematology", and "ECG" activities are performed. Besides, for MUMC the "corneal topography", "retina OCT", and "biometry" tests are typically performed together. For both hospitals the process starts with a first visit.

Observation 2 (O2):   Here for both hospitals the process is the same. First, the patient is admitted ("admission hospital"). Then the surgical procedure takes place ("cataract surgery with lens"). Finally, the patient is discharged again ("discharge hospital").

Observation 3 (O3):   At AMC a patient typically only visits the outpatient clinic multiple times ("next visit OC" activity) in the aftercare trajectory. This activity is also performed at MUMC during this trajectory. However, it may also be the case that a patient visits the emergency care department ("emergency care" activity) of MUMC. Also, some diagnostic tests may be performed ("corneal topography" and "retina OCT" activities).

To "quantify" the extent of the observed differences, we replayed each hospital's log on the Petri net models of the two hospitals. The cost-based fitness metric [7] for each replay was calculated, the results of which are shown in Table 5.1. In this way, we find how much comparable the processes of the two hospitals are. The fitness of

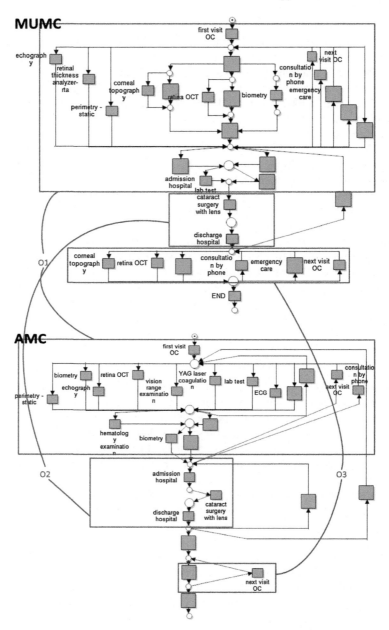

Fig. 5.13 Discovered processes for MUMC and AMC. Differences are coded as "O1", "O2", and "O3"

Table 5.1 Fitness values for the various logs and discovered models of the two hospitals

	Process Model (Petri Net)	
Hospital log	H1	H2
MUMC (H1)	0.92	0.76
AMC (H2)	0.65	0.86

a model describes how well a model conforms to the log. For example, if the fitness is "1" then all traces can be successfully replayed in the model whereas a fitness of "0" indicates that none of the traces can be successfully replayed.

When replaying the MUMC-log in the AMC model and the AMC-log in the MUMC model the fitness is 0.76 and 0.65 respectively. As such, the processes of the MUMC and AMC are quite comparable. Basically, they follow the same structure but only differ in some activities that are performed. Altogether, this kind of analysis shows that for two hospitals with the same patient group the process can be compared thereby revealing the difference in activities that are performed.

5.3.6 Use Case 6: Context-Aware Process Mining

Process mining discovers process knowledge based on an event log. For a discovered process model it may be interesting to discover additional process knowledge based on the additional data available in the event log. This additional knowledge can be discovered using data mining. For example, it can be investigated which trace features have an impact on trace fitness, i.e., the fitness between a given trace and a model. Does a higher patient age lead to a lower trace fitness or do urgent patients typically have a lower trace fitness?

We illustrate this log by studying the AMC's cataract process as shown at the bottom of Fig. 5.13. More specifically, we predict the fitness for each patient trace based on several patient characteristics. Additional AMC data had to be gathered for this purpose. Figure 5.14a shows the additional classes of the reference model for which data was obtained. Furthermore, in Fig. 5.14b a snippet of the data are shown. For example, patient "p1" is female, has age "74", the surgery isn't urgent, and the patient was admitted to the daycare center. Also, the fitness between the discovered model and the patient's trace was high, and the number of events before surgery was "8". Note that the "fitness category" and the "# events surgery" have been added by us. In Fig. 5.14, the discovered decision tree can be seen. This tree is obtained by applying a decision tree learner that classifies both nominal and numerical data. The aim of the learner is to create a classification model that predicts the value of a target attribute based on several input attributes of a data set. In our case, the value of the fitness category is predicted based on the other attributes in the data set. For example, in the resultant decision tree, it can be seen that if the age is "63" or lower and the number of events before surgery is lower than 8 then in general the fitness is

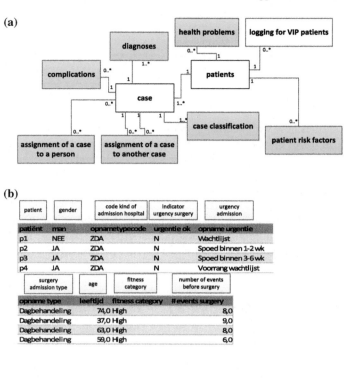

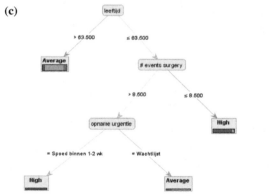

Fig. 5.14 Data that have been collected for AMC's cataract patients. Furthermore, the decision tree that has been obtained for the data set is shown. **a** Overview of the classes of the 'general patient and case data' group for which data has been obtained for the AMC hospital. By using this data, additional knowledge about a discovered process model can be obtained. **b** Snippet of the data that has been obtained for the patient and case classes of the 'general patient and case data' group, the *movements for case* class of the 'process steps' group and the *surgery* class of the 'document data' group. (Figs. 4.2, 4.4, and 4.12). **c** Resultant decision tree. For example, if the age is 63.5 or lower and the number of events before surgery is lower than 8.5 then in general the fitness is high

high. Finally, the performance of the classification has accuracy 79.5 %.[2] To test the quality of the overall model cross validation can be used. So, altogether, the fitness type can be well predicted by the age, the number of events before surgery, and the urgency of the admission. This kind of analysis made clear for which types of patients, the process model is typically not followed.

5.3.7 Outlook

The above described use cases illustrate the kinds of analysis that are possible with process mining. The six use cases can be chained together in so-called composite use cases. These composite uses cases correspond to realistic types of analysis. However, this does not mean that other kinds of process mining analyses are not possible. ProM 6 contains plug-ins for many of the recently developed algorithms in the process mining field [8, 9]. For example, for a process it is possible to check its compliance regarding temporal rules [10] (e.g. it is checked whether after a visit to the outpatient clinic always a lab test is performed within 24 h). Also, it is possible to repair a process model with regard to a log such that the resulting model can replay the log (i.e., conforms to it) and is as similar as possible to the original model [11]. For example, using the event log it is found that between a visit to the outpatient clinic and a chemotherapy always a lab test is performed. Subsequently, the process model is adapted in order to represent this behavior.

However, other kinds of analysis and functionalities using process mining are offered via *RapidProM*.[3] RapidProM integrates ProM 6 within the advanced analytics software tool RapidMiner[4] [12]. Moreover, RapidMiner allows for the definition and execution of analysis workflows. As a result of this integration, several advantages are realized. First, any discovery, conformance, or extension algorithm of ProM can be used within a RapidMiner analysis process thus supporting process mining workflows. Second, comparable process mining analyses can be repeated by just one-click of a button and scientific experiments can be executed in an automated fashion. Finally, within RapidMiner many data and machine learning techniques are readily available. As such, different techniques can be easily combined for an end-to-end analysis. An example of such an analysis is that by means of a decision tree analysis it is discovered for which values of data attributes a certain path of the decision point has been taken. Another example is that an experiment is set up in which a selection of process models is obtained together with some quality measures. In this way, it is possible to select a process model which scores best against these measures.

---

[2] The classification indicates the percentage of correct predictions.

[3] www.rapidprom.org.

[4] www.rapidminer.org.

References

1. M.S. Song and W.M.P. van der Aalst. Supporting Process Mining by Showing Events at a Glance. In K Chari and A Kumar, editors, *Proceedings of the Seventeenth Annual Workshop on Information Technologies and Systems (WITS 2007)*, pages 139–145, 2007
2. W.M.P. van der Aalst. *Process Mining: Discovery, Conformance and Enhancement of Business Processes*. Springer-Verlag, Berlin, 2011
3. C.W. Günther and W.M.P. van der Aalst. Fuzzy Mining: Adaptive Process Simplification Based on Multi-perspective Metrics. In *International Conference on Business Process Management (BPM 2007)*, volume 4714 of *Lecture Notes in Computer Science*, pages 328–343. Springer-Verlag, Berlin, 2007
4. R.P. Jagadeesh Chandra Bose and W.M.P. van der Aalst. Process Diagnostics using Trace Alignment: Opportunities, Issues, and Challenges. *Information Systems*, 37(2): 117–141, 2012
5. A. Rozinat and W.M.P. van der Aalst. Decision Mining in ProM. In S Dustdar, J L Fiadeiro, and A Sheth, editors, *BPM 2006*, volume 4102 of *Lecture Notes in Computer Science*, pages 420–425. Springer-Verlag, Berlin, 2006
6. W.M.P. van der Aalst, H.T. de Beer, and B.F. van Dongen. Process Mining and Verification of Properties: An Approach based on Temporal Logic. In R Meersman and Z Tari Et al., editors, *On the Move to Meaningful Internet Systems 2005: CoopIS, DOA, and ODBASE: OTM Confederated International Conferences, CoopIS, DOA, and ODBASE 2005*, volume 3760 of *Lecture Notes in Computer Science*, pages 130–147. Springer-Verlag, Berlin, 2005
7. W.M.P. van der Aalst, A. Adriansyah, and B.F. van Dongen. Replaying History on Process Models for Conformance Checking and Performance Analysis. *WIREs Data Mining and Knowledge Discovery*, 2(2): 182–192, 2012
8. H.M.W. Verbeek, J.C.A.M. Buijs, B.F. van Dongen, and W.M.P. van der Aalst. ProM 6: The Process Mining Toolkit. In *Proc. of BPM Demonstration Track 2010*, volume 615, pages 34–39. CEUR-WS.org, 2010
9. H.M.W. Verbeek, J.C.A.M. Buijs, B.F. van Dongen, and W.M.P. van der Aalst. XES, XESame, and ProM 6. In *Information Systems Evolution*, volume 72 of *Lecture Notes in Computer Science*, pages 60–75. Springer Verlag Berlin-Heidelberg, 2011
10. E. Ramezani, D. Fahland, B.F. van Dongen, and W.M.P. van der Aalst. Diagnostic Information for Compliance Checking of Temporal Compliance Requirements. In C. Salinesi, M.C. Norrie, and O. Pastor, editors, *Advanced Information Systems Engineering (25th International Conference, CAiSE 2013, Valencia, Spain, June 17–21, 2013. Proceedings)*, volume 7908 of *Lecture Notes in Computer Science*, pages 304–320, 2013
11. D. Fahland and W.M.P. van der Aalst. Model Repair - Aligning Process Models to Reality. *Information Systems*, 2014. submitted / in press
12. R.S. Mans, W.M.P. van der Aalst, and H.M.W. Verbeek. Supporting Process Mining Workflows with RapidProM. In *To appear in Proceeding of BPM Demonstration Track 2014*, 2014

Chapter 6
Data Quality Issues

Abstract Healthcare data, like any data, may have all kinds of quality problems. In this chapter, we identify 27 data quality issues that may compromise the validity of process mining results. Examples are missing data, incorrect data, imprecise data, and irrelevant data. For example, an event may only have a date (e.g., 15-6-2015) and not a fine-grained timestamp. As a result, the ordering of events is unknown, thus complicating analysis. Practitioners were interviewed to estimate the frequency of the 27 types of data quality issues identified. This provides insights into typical problems that may arise in data-science projects in hospitals. The quality of the analysis results directly depends on the input data (i.e., Garbage-In Garbage-Out). Therefore, the chapter also discusses 12 guidelines for logging. These guidelines should be used when developing the next generation of hospital information systems. Improved event logs will enable more advanced forms of process mining related to prediction and recommendation.

Keywords Guidelines of logging · Data quality · Hospital information systems · Process mining · Event data · XES · Healthcare

So far, we have introduced our *healthcare reference model* and demonstrated some examples of process mining possibilities. While doing this, we did not consider data quality issues, i.e., the data are available and correct. However, in reality we need to cope with many data quality issues [1, 2]. In order to obtain reliable and trustful process mining results it is important that the analyst is aware of the data quality issues that may manifest in a HIS and that may negatively impact the reliability and value of process mining analysis. Therefore, we investigate in this section which kinds of data quality issues may exist for the data that is part of the *healthcare reference model*. In order to identify these data issues, the following approach is taken. In [1], 27 data quality issues are presented which may complicate the creation of a suitable and trustworthy event log. For the data present in the HIS of the MUMC, we investigate which of the 27 quality issues indeed correspond to problems in the data set analyzed. Finally, in order to increase the quality of data in a HIS, we elaborate on a set of guidelines for the logging of event data [2]. By following these guidelines the quality of event logs will increase and more powerful and reliable process mining analyses can be performed.

© The Author(s) 2015
R.S. Mans et al., *Process Mining in Healthcare*,
SpringerBriefs in Business Process Management, DOI 10.1007/978-3-319-16071-9_6

In Sect. 6.1 we briefly introduce the data quality issues that were identified in [1]. In Sect. 6.2, the classification of such issues is used for evaluating the data that is present in the HIS of the MUMC. Finally, in Sect. 6.3, the guidelines of logging are discussed.

6.1 Classification of Event Log Quality Issues

In [1], in total 27 event data related quality issues that may occur within an event log were identified. The following four classes of broad problem types can be distinguished. Note that the issues defined in [1] relate specifically to an event log. However, it is trivial to generalize these issues from a single event log to the event data stored in a HIS.

- **Missing Data**: Different kinds of process mining information are *missing* although the information is mandatory. For example, an event, a process instance, or an attribute/value of an event may be missing.
- **Incorrect Data**: Although process mining data may be provided, it may be the case that the provided information is logged *incorrectly*. For example, for the timestamp of an event an impossible value was recorded.
- **Imprecise Data**: The information that is logged is too coarse leading to a *loss of precision*. As result, certain kinds of analysis are not possible anymore as a more precise value is needed in order to obtain reliable results. For example, the timestamps that are logged for certain events may be too coarse (e.g., in the order of a day) thereby making the ordering of events unreliable.
- **Irrelevant Data**: When considering the information that has been logged, the information *as it is* may be considered irrelevant for analysis. However, it may be possible to derive/obtain another relevant entity (e.g., through filtering/aggregation) from the logged entities. For example, for a certain analysis knowing that a lab test is performed might be sufficient. Information with regard to the underlying individual lab tests may be considered superfluous.

The four classes of problems hold for different concepts within an event log. To this end, in Fig. 6.1 we show the typical information that is present in an event log. Note that this figure has already been described in detail in Sect. 3.1. However, in order to understand the remainder of this chapter, a part of this description is repeated. If needed, additional information is given.

An event log captures the execution of a *process*. As part of this, for the process, multiple *cases* are stored. For each case, multiple *attributes* may be stored such as case id, etc. Each case consists of an ordered list of *events*. As an event can only belong to one case only it is explicitly stored to which case an event belongs. This is defined by the *relationship* relation. For an event, it is mandatory that it refers to an activity or task. Note that in our case, an event may for example refer to a service, a movement, or an event that occurred (the movements for case, services

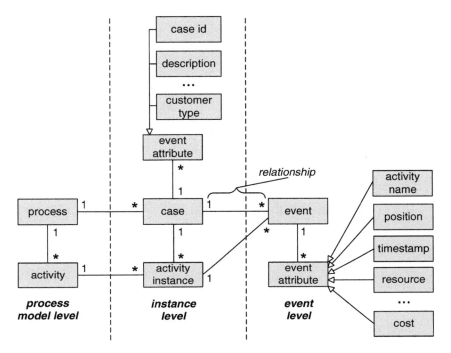

Fig. 6.1 The typical information that needs to be present in an event log. Additionally, the relation between a process model and a event log is depicted

`performed`, and `occurred events` classes in Fig. 4.4). Therefore, always a value needs to be provided for the *activity name* attribute of an event. Next to that, an event may have optional attributes such as a *timestamp*, *position*, *resource*, or other attributes. Note that it is important that events within a case are ordered. This ordering is either determined by the timestamp attribute or the position attribute which specifies the index of an event in a case.

Table 6.1 shows the manifestation of the four classes of problems across the different entities of an event log. Note that "c_attribute" refers to an attribute of a case and "e_attribute" refers to an attribute of an event. In this way, 27 different quality issues have been identified. For each issue an unique number has been given with prefix "I". For example, the "missing data" quality issue for the "relationship" concept of the log (I3) corresponds to the scenario where the association between events and case are missing. Furthermore, the "imprecise data" quality issue for the "timestamp" concept (I23) corresponds to the scenario where timestamps are imprecise since a coarse level of abstraction is used for the timestamps of (some of the) events. As a result, the ordering of events within a case may be unreliable. For a detailed discussion of all the identified quality issues, we refer to [1].

Table 6.1 For each concept within an event log it is indicated whether the "missing", "incorrect", "imprecise", and "irrelevant" problem type is possible

	Case	Event	Relationship	c_attribute	Position	Activity name	Timestamp	Resource	e_attribute
Missing data	I1	I2	I3	I4	I5	I6	I7	I8	I9
Incorrect data	I10	I11	I12	I13	I14	I15	I16	I17	I18
Imprecise data			I19	I20	I21	I22	I23	I24	I25
Irrelevant data	I26	I27							

For example, "I23" refers to imprecise timestamps, e.g., events have a date but no precise timestamp

6.2 Evaluation of Data Quality Issues

In this section, the 27 event log quality issues listed in Table 6.1 are used for evaluating the data that is present in the HIS of the MUMC. This evaluation is used to illustrate the kinds of process mining related data quality issues that may occur in a hospital.

In order to identify the data quality issues that occur for the *i.s.h.med* system in use at the MUMC, we interviewed people within the hospital which have knowledge about the raw data that is present in the system. Moreover, we inspected tables in the database ourselves in order to identify possible quality issues. Our evaluation is subjective but due to the large amount of data present in the entire system we consider it infeasible that an objective evaluation is performed. Moreover, for some quality issues it is difficult to obtain objective measures (e.g., the amount of events that are missing).

More specifically, we focused on identifying quality issues whose occurrence is more frequent than the occurrence of other data quality issues. In this way, we identify the issues that are the most prominent. As shown in Table 6.2, for each quality issue we distinguish three different values. The character "N" indicates that the quality issue does not occur. An "L" means that the quality issue may be present but does not occur frequently. A value "H" indicates that a quality problem occurs more frequently, i.e., it is more prominent compared to other issues. Finally, the box associated to a quality issue is left empty if the quality issue does not apply. For example, as each entry in the HIS of the MUMC is relevant for a certain patient, the irrelevant data quality issues do not apply. Below, the quality issues to which an "L" or an "H" are assigned, are briefly discussed.

- **Missing Events (I2), value H**: Many events need to be entered manually into the system. As a result, during our discussions we identified that one of the most prominent problems in the HIS is that people forget to enter services although they were performed in reality.
- **Missing Relationship (I3), value L**: In principle, every event needs to be linked to a case. However, in the system there were events which were not linked to a case but it is expected that its frequency is low. For example, for the table associated to the services that were performed for patients (class `services performed` in Fig. 4.4) in total 67,295,460 events are registered. For 17,568 of them (approximately 0.03 %) no associated case is stored.
- **Missing Case Attributes (I4), value L**: Also for the case attributes it holds that they need to be entered manually into the system. However, it is expected that, compared to the recording of the events (data quality issue I2), the quality of the recorded case attributes is better.
- **Missing Activity Name (I6), value L**: Although for each event an activity name needs to be provided it may occur that this does not happen in reality. As a result of our discussions with data experts of the MUMC it is expected that its occurrence is low. For example, regarding the services that have been performed for patients (class `services performed` in Fig. 4.4), there are only 84 events for which no activity name has been provided.

Table 6.2 Evaluation of data quality issues for the *i.s.h.med* system in use at the MUMC

	Case	Event	Relationship	c_attribute	Position	Activity name	Timestamp	Resource	e_attribute
Missing data	N	H	L	L	N	L	N	N	L
Incorrect data	N	L	L	L	N	L	L	N	L
Imprecise data			N	N	N	N	H	H	N
Irrelevant data									

In case a quality issue is not applicable, the corresponding box is left empty. The value *N* indicates that the issue does not occur. Furthermore, an *L* indicates that a quality issue occurs relatively infrequently whereas an "H" indicates that an issue occurs more frequently in comparison with other issues

- **Missing Timestamp (I7), value L**: Also regarding timestamps it may happen that no value is registered. However, in many cases a timestamp is recorded automatically by the system itself. Therefore, experts of the MUMC expected that the occurrence of this quality issue is low.
- **Missing Event Attribute (I9), value L**: Analogously to the case attributes, a low frequency of occurrence is expected.
- **Incorrect Event (I11), value L**: By incident an event may be recorded for a patient which did not happen in reality. Here, it is anticipated in the hospital that its occurrence is low.
- **Incorrect Case Attribute (I13), value L**: For a case attribute it may always be the case that a wrong value was entered. However, during our discussions it was expected that this should be quite exceptional. Therefore, the value "L" is provided as evaluation.
- **Incorrect Activity Name (I15), value L**: In the system, events are found which are unlikely regarding the illness for which a patient is treated. For example, instead of a CT-abdomen it is recorded that a CT-scan of the foot has been made. This kind of quality issue is not expected to occur frequently.
- **Incorrect Timestamp (I16), value L**: The entire system contains a wealth of timestamp information. As already indicated before, many of the timestamps are automatically saved as part of a record that is saved in the system. However, there are also records for which the associated timestamp is saved by hand. For example, regarding the services that have been performed for patients (class `services performed` in Fig. 4.4), there are 124 of the 67,295,460 events (0.0001 %) which have "31.12.2020" as associated timestamp. This quality issue is not expected to occur frequently.
- **Incorrect Event Attribute (I18), value L**: For an event attribute it can always be the case that a wrong value has been given. Similar to the "incorrect case attribute" data quality issue a low frequency is expected.
- **Imprecise Timestamp (I23), value H**: Within the hospital there are several medical disciplines which use their own dedicated system for the medical services they perform. In order for the hospital to be reimbursed for these services, they are imported afterwards into the *i.s.h.med* system. During this import only the day is saved on which the services have been performed. As this is the case for a considerable group of events, the evaluation "H" is given. For example, regarding the radiology department and pathology departments there are 636,363 and 664,675 services stored with only a day timestamp. Note that in the dedicated systems of these departments more precise timestamp information is available.
- **Imprecise Resource (I24), value H**: In the system for each action it is saved which resource recorded it. However, in some cases the saved resource may not refer to a specific person. For example, regarding the services that have been performed for patients (class `services performed` in Fig. 4.4), there are 234,378 of the 67,295,460 events (0.3 %) for which the recorded resource refers to a specific operating room instead of the person who performed the surgery. This issue tends to occur more frequently compared to other issues.

The discussion above makes clear that the HIS of the MUMC suffers from several of the data quality issues described in [1]. Moreover, given our experiences with process mining in healthcare, these issues are also very likely to occur for other HIS implementations. Given the existence of these issues, it is important that they are detected and properly handled (e.g., by applying repair techniques in order to alleviate these issues). Some process mining techniques exist which are able to deal with some quality issues (e.g., the fuzzy miner [3] and the heuristics miner are able to handle missing events [4]). Also, in [5] several methods are given for detecting time related quality issues.

Despite data quality issues that may apply, process mining is still possible. For example, events or cases for which issues may exist can easily be filtered. As a result, many analyses are still possible and many interesting insights can be obtained.

6.3 Improving Data Quality: Guidelines of Logging

The data quality problems just described illustrate that the input side of analytics (process mining, data mining, etc.) is often neglected [2]. Event data are often seen as a by-product. For example, the data are there for financial reasons or simply because a programmer decide to put a write statement in the code. Since the "input side of process mining" is vital, we now discuss the *twelve guidelines for logging* introduced in [2]. These guidelines make no assumptions on the underlying technology used to record event data.

In this section, we use a rather loose definition of event data: events simply refer to "things that happen" and are described by *references* and *attributes*. *References* have a *reference name* and an *identifier* that refers to some object (person, case, ticket, machine, room, etc.) in the universe of discourse. *Attributes* have a *name* and a *value*, e.g., $age = 48$ or $time =$ "*19-11-2014 03:14:00*". Based on these concepts we define our twelve guidelines. To create an event log from such "raw events"

- we need to select the events relevant for the process at hand,
- events need to be correlated to process instances,
- events need to be ordered using timestamp information, and
- event attributes need to be selected or computed based on the raw data (resource, cost, etc.).

As we have seen in the previous chapter, such an event log can be used as input for a wealth of process-mining techniques.

The guidelines for logging (**GL1–GL12**) aim to create a good starting point for process mining [2].

GL1   *Reference and attribute names should have clear semantics, i.e., they should have the same meaning for all people involved in creating and analyzing event data.* Different stakeholders should interpret event data in the same way.

GL2   *There should be a structured and managed collection of reference and attribute names.* Ideally, names are grouped hierarchically (like a taxonomy or ontology). A new reference or attribute name can only be added after there is consensus on its value and meaning. Also consider adding domain or organization specific extensions (see for example the extension mechanism of XES [6]).

GL3   *References should be stable (e.g., identifiers should not be reused or rely on the context).* For example, references should not be time, region, or language dependent. Some systems create different logs depending on the language settings. This is unnecessarily complicating analysis.

GL4   *Attribute values should be as precise as possible. If the value does not have the desired precision, this should be indicated explicitly (e.g., through a qualifier).* For example, if for some events only the date is known but not the exact timestamp, then this should be stated explicitly.

GL5   *Uncertainty with respect to the occurrence of the event or its references or attributes should be captured through appropriate qualifiers.* For example, due to communication errors, some values may be less reliable than usual. Note that uncertainty is different from imprecision.

GL6   *Events should be at least partially ordered. The ordering of events may be stored explicitly (e.g., using a list) or implicitly through an attribute denoting the event's timestamp.* If the recording of timestamps is unreliable or imprecise, there may still be ways to order events based on observed causalities (e.g., usage of data).

GL7   *If possible, also store transactional information about the event (start, complete, abort, schedule, assign, suspend, resume, withdraw, etc.).* Having start and complete events allows for the computation of activity durations. It is recommended to store activity references to be able to relate events belonging to the same activity instance. Without activity references it may not always be clear which events belong together, which start event corresponds to which complete event.

GL8   *Perform regularly automated consistency and correctness checks to ensure the syntactical correctness of the event log.* Check for missing references or attributes, and reference/attribute names not agreed upon. Event quality assurance is a continuous process (to avoid degradation of log quality over time).

GL9   *Ensure comparability of event logs over time and different groups of cases or process variants.* The logging itself should not change over time (without being reported). For comparative process mining, it is vital that the same logging principles are used. If for some groups of cases, some events are not recorded even though they occur, then this may suggest differences that do not actually exist.

GL10   *Do not aggregate events in the event log used as input for the analysis process.* Aggregation should be done during analysis and not before (since it cannot be undone). Event data should be as "raw" as possible.

GL11   *Do not remove events and ensure provenance. Reproducibility is key for process mining.* For example, do not remove a student from the database after he dropped out since this may lead to misleading analysis results. Mark objects as not relevant (a so-called "soft delete") rather than deleting them: concerts are not deleted—they are canceled, employees are not deleted—they are fired, etc.

GL12   *Ensure privacy without losing meaningful correlations.* Sensitive or private data should be removed as early as possible (i.e., before analysis). However, if possible, one should avoid removing correlations. For example, it is often not useful to know the name of a student, but it may be important to still be able to use his high school marks and know what other courses he failed. Hashing can be a powerful tool in the trade-off between privacy and analysis.

The above guidelines are very general and aim to improve the logging itself. It is clear that they try to overcome the 27 quality issues described in the first half of this chapter.

6.4   Garbage-In Garbage-Out

In Chap. 4 a healthcare reference model was given that describes the typical data one can find in a hospital. Assuming there are no data quality issues and the information is indeed present, an array of process mining techniques can be applied. Chapter 5 could only show the tip of the iceberg of possibilities. Compliance and performance can be improved using process mining. However, the data quality issues discussed in Sect. 6.1 clearly complicate matters. The quality of the analysis results directly depends on the input data (Garbage-In Garbage-Out). Therefore, we presented twelve guidelines for logging (Sect. 6.3). These are not only important for process mining. The application of any data science technique in hospitals will stand or fall with high-quality data. *Event data are not just a byproduct of operational processes: They are the fuel for process improvement!*

References

1. R. P. Jagadeesh Chandra Bose, R.S. Mans, and W.M.P. van der Aalst. Wanna Improve Process Mining Results? – It's High Time We Consider Data Quality Issues Seriously. BPM Center Report BPM-13-02, BPMcenter.org, 2013
2. W.M.P. van der Aalst. Extracting Event Data from Databases to Unleash Process Mining. In J. Vom Brocke and T. Schmiedel, editors, *Business Process Management Roundtable 2014*, pages 1–25. Springer, 2014
3. C.W. Günther and W.M.P. van der Aalst. Fuzzy Mining: Adaptive Process Simplification Based on Multi-perspective Metrics. In *International Conference on Business Process Management (BPM 2007)*, volume 4714 of *Lecture Notes in Computer Science*, pages 328–343. Springer-Verlag, Berlin, 2007
4. W.M.P. van der Aalst. *Process Mining: Discovery, Conformance and Enhancement of Business Processes*. Springer-Verlag, Berlin, 2011
5. M.L. van Eck. Timestamps Within Healthcare Process Mining Logs. Master's thesis, Eindhoven University of Technology, Eindhoven, 2013
6. IEEE Task Force on Process Mining. XES Standard Definition. www.xes-standard.org, 2013

Chapter 7
Epilogue

Abstract To address challenges related to efficiency and costs in healthcare, we need to exploit the event data present in today's hospital information systems. Recent developments in data science are an important enabler for providing better and cheaper healthcare solutions. The healthcare reference model and the guidelines for logging aim to improve the input side, i.e., the goal is to collect high-quality event data. However, it is not enough to collect torrents of data. Powerful analysis techniques are needed to analyze the behavioral aspects of care processes. In this *SpringerBrief*, we proposed process mining as a key technology for understanding and improving healthcare processes. There are process-mining techniques to analyze bottlenecks, to uncover hidden inefficiencies, to check compliance, to explain deviations, to predict performance, and to guide users toward better care processes. This chapter summarizes the main contributions of this *SpringerBrief*.

Keywords Process mining · Healthcare · Hospital information systems

Today's hospitals record an abundance of event data. Moreover, it is expected that in the future much more high quality event data will become available. Therefore, data science will play an increasingly important role in the improvement of healthcare processes. Process mining provides the tools to exploit the types of data described in this *SpringerBrief*. In the remainder we briefly summarize our findings.

In Chaps. 2 and 3 we focused on different kinds of processes that exist in healthcare and gave an introduction to process mining. One of the big advantages of process mining is that analysis is based on *facts* rather than fiction. The process models that are manually created in organizations are typically only used for documentation and communication purposes and therefore tend to present a "PowerPoint" reality. Moreover, people involved in the performance of these healthcare processes (e.g. physicians, managers) typically only have a limited, biased or idealized view on how these processes are executed. That is, they tend to have particular scenarios in mind thereby abstracting away relevant alternative scenarios. By using process mining, it can be seen how healthcare processes are *really* executed. It is an ideal tool to go from political to more analytical discussions.

© The Author(s) 2015   89
R.S. Mans et al., *Process Mining in Healthcare*,
SpringerBriefs in Business Process Management, DOI 10.1007/978-3-319-16071-9_7

In Chap. 4, we presented a *healthcare reference model* outlining for a hospital all the different classes of data that are potentially available for process mining together with the relationships between these classes. Without such a model it is difficult to reason about questions that may or may not be answered using process mining. Moreover, the model is instrumental in locating the data needed and facilitating the actual execution, Another advantage is that the reference model creates an *awareness* of all the data that is present within the hospital. Based on this, many logs can be generated each focusing on different (parts of) processes.

Chapter 5 described different applications of process mining in healthcare. The presented use cases made clear that the following kinds of analyses (and many more) can be performed:

1. Exploring selections of events such that the scoping of the analysis becomes clear.
2. Identifying and quantifying deviations in order to investigate deviations between an event log and the model that describes how the process needs to be executed.
3. Identifying and quantifying bottlenecks in order to find performance related problems within the process.
4. Drilling down into the data according to different dimensions in order to analyze a (part of a) process in more detail.
5. Comparing processes of different hospitals such that differences in terms of activities and the ordering of activities can be identified.
6. Classifying event log data such that additional process knowledge can be obtained using a combination of models and data.

Moreover, the use cases made clear that, by following the classification in Chap. 2, different kinds of processes can be analyzed. Also, comparable processes of different organizations can be compared and it is possible to deal with recorded process steps residing at different levels of granularity. Next to that, process mining should not be used in isolation but results can be enriched by applying techniques from the data mining and machine learning domains. Techniques from these domains can be used for discovering additional process knowledge based on the data that is present in an event log. The website http://www.healthcare-analytics-process-mining.org describes more case studies.

Finally, before applying process mining at all, an analyst should be aware of the fact that an event log may have all kinds of quality issues. To this end, we classified such issues in Chap. 6. We also showed that these data quality issues are indeed presents in today's hospital information systems. These issues need to be taken into account during process mining analysis in order to obtain reliable results. Moreover, twelve guidelines for logging have been presented in an effort to avoid such problems in future information systems.

Alltogether, there are plenty of reasons for using process mining in healthcare. The obtained insights can serve as a basis for improving or governing healthcare processes such that these are performed more efficiently and effectively. In that way, process mining can really contribute to the improvement of healthcare processes. This is needed because of rising costs and an aging society. We need to be able to do more with less people. The healthcare reference model shows that lots of event data are there. These are waiting to be analyzed using process mining. Moreover, powerful tools such as ProM 6[1] and RapidProM[2] are freely available. Hence, there is no excuse: *Start applying process mining to your healthcare data today!*

---

[1] www.processmining.org.

[2] www.rapidprom.org.

Printed by Printforce, the Netherlands